Beekeeping for Beginners

A Step-By-Step Guide to Building Your First Beehive

Janet Wilson

Copyright © 2020 by Janet Wilson

ALL RIGHTS RESERVED

No part of this book may be reproduced, stored in a retrieval system, or transmitted in any form or by any means, electronic, mechanical, photocopying, recording, scanning, or otherwise, without the prior written permission of the publisher.

Limit of Liability/Disclaimer of Warranty: the publisher and the author make no representations or warranties with respect to the accuracy or completeness of the contents of this work and specifically disclaim all warranties, including without limitation warranties of fitness for a particular purpose. No warranty may be created or extended by sales or promotional materials. The advice and strategies contained herein may not be suitable for every situation. This work is sold with the understanding that the publisher is not engaged in rendering medical, legal or other professional advice or services. If professional assistance is required, the services of a competent professional person should be sought. Neither the publisher nor the author shall be liable for damages arising herefrom. The fact that an individual, organization or website is referred to in this work as a citation and/or potential source of further information does not mean that the author or the publisher endorses the information the individuals, organization or website may provide or recommendations they/it may make. Further, readers should be aware that websites listed on this work may have changed or disappeared between when this work was written and when it is read. **ISBN: 978-1-951791-50-6**

Get Your Free Checklist:

- Learn How To Build Your Own Tiny House
- Includes Tiny House Plans
- Access to a Private Sustainable Living Community

Visit:

Janetwilson.org

Table of Contents

Introduction 5
Chapter One: Essential Ideas of Beekeeping................................ 7
Chapter Two: Preparing Your Hive.. 20
Chapter Three: Introducing the Bees to The Hive....................... 31
Chapter Four: Feeding and Nurturing Bees................................. 46
Chapter Five: Beekeeping Seasons... 56
Chapter Six: All About the Harvest.. 70
Chapter Seven: Handling Parasites, Predators, and Diseases...... 80
Chapter Eight: Essential Beekeeping Supplies for Beginners..... 93
Chapter Nine: Beekeeping Cleaning Procedures........................ 102
Chapter Ten: Beekeeping Mistakes to Avoid.............................. 114
Final Words 131

Introduction

Who doesn't love honey? Think about the millions of people who rely on honey for varying health reasons: yes, honey is king, but before getting it, one has to get to the bees that make it. Beekeeping is the nurturing process that leads to the harvesting of honey. But there is so much more to beekeeping than honey, and you are about to unravel all the details in this book.

The idea of nurturing bees doesn't appeal to everyone. Some people are naturally only interested in getting the end product (honey), while some others seek to enjoy the process that leads to this result. If you do belong to the latter group, then this volume will provide a great deal of comprehensive and detailed material on beekeeping for beginners.

In this book, you will find details about the first beekeeping steps to take and how to prepare your hive for the bees. You will also gain insight into the ideal beekeeping seasons, harvesting your bees, and honey extraction.

A significant reason why some people stay away from beekeeping is the vulnerability of bees to predators and diseases. Well, here you will learn how to protect your hive from such predators, the preventive measures to put in place, as well as common beekeeping mistakes to avoid. Think about this book as a

"Beekeeping bible" that will instill confidence in you to handle the beekeeping process the right way.

Now, the fact that you are learning in the most simplified, yet comprehensive way doesn't mean the process is a walk in a park. Along with other positive ventures, beekeeping requires a lot of work and paying attention to the tiniest details. As such, even as you read this book, please remember that it is only a worthwhile experience when you give it your best.

This book's objective is to introduce you to the core concepts and inspire you to take action as you read. For some people, beekeeping is an idea to be executed only by "Professionals," hence the reason they are reluctant to try. But think about this, how did professional beekeepers become successful? The answer is simple: they took the first step and never looked back!

You are taking your first step now, but the question is, will you be committed to the process? Will you maximize all you learn by baby steps until you become a professional? If yes, then you are ready to take on this project, and I will be with you from the beginning until the end. Let us begin with the first and foundational chapter that introduces you to the world of beekeeping: it promises to be just as sweet as honey!

Chapter One:
Essential Ideas of Beekeeping

Beekeeping is also known as apiculture, which refers to the maintenance of bee colonies commonly known as human-made hives. Through this process, honeybees are nurtured in an environment that will help them thrive enough to produce honey and other products collected from the colony, including beeswax, flower pollen, royal jelly, etc.

One of the most common aims of beekeeping is to ensure one nurtures large and healthy adult honeybee populations that produce large amounts of nectar flow. To do this, you need healthy bee colonies, and you need to implement proper beekeeping management. Beekeeping also provides pollination services for local crops; this can provide an income for some beekeepers as well as the more obvious opportunities to sell the products they make from the bees.

Beekeeping is not a new concept; it has been a long-term practice with historical antecedents traced to ancient Egypt, Greece, and China. From those past times until now, beekeeping has become a prevalent practice across the world, with people growing beehives for both commercial and personal purposes.

This book is tailored to suit the expectations of both groups of people: those who want to grow bees for commercial purposes and those who want to do it for personal purposes. Through this book, you will unravel the primary and fundamental concepts about beekeeping that will help you start the process.

Now, generally, you should know that beekeeping, just like every other animal nurturing process, demands a lot of time and attention. From building your hives, to getting the bees and keeping the hive safe before harvest time, you will need time and dedication. The subsequent chapters and sections below will show you what to do, but before you get there, let's unravel the foundational aspects of beekeeping.

Honeybees are insects that live in colonies led by a queen bee; the insects can be dangerous sometimes when provoked as they can inflict harsh stings on a person's body. Even before getting to the main aspects of our discourse, you should know the necessary precautions to take when dealing with bees.

Bees also produce their own food: honey. They feed on nectar during inclement weather that is not favorable to them (these are times when they cannot go out). In the world today, honey is a viable and very precious commodity because of its taste and health benefits. There are diverse ways of nurturing bees from infancy to adult stages.

Modern beehives also aid in the faster production of honey and the collection of bee products. This modernized process of beekeeping enables the continuous protection of the bee colony even after the products are harvested. So, what are the benefits of being a beekeeper? Are there particular challenges to this venture? What about the factors to consider?

In the sections below, I will strike a balance with the introductory narrative by showing you both the benefit of beekeeping and some of the beehive products you can harvest through this process. You will also find ideas on some challenges you may encounter and the appropriate solutions.

Beehive Products That Can Be Harvested

Honey

Of course, honey is the first and most important product you will get from your beehive, and the more attention you give to the colony, the more honey you will harvest. As you go further on this journey, you will find more interesting facts about honey and the reason why it is one of the most sought-after nutritional products in the world.

Beeswax

After honey, the bee wax is the second most essential bee product: aside from the fact that human beings use it, bees also use the wax to build their hive structures. The structures are called "Honeycombs" shaped like a hexagonal cell. One part of the honeycomb has thousands of cells, and since a typical honeycomb is two-sided, you will find a great deal of beeswax on them.

Pollen

Pollen is also a beehive product that has gained popularity in the modern beekeeping world. Pollen is used in various ways, but mainly as a health-boosting food supplement as it is rich in protein. Pollen is collected from flowers by hunting honeybees and then stored inside the beehive in a granular form. Pollen is also used as food for the queen bee and larvae inside the hive (other bees may eat it occasionally).

Royal jelly

The royal jelly is a paste-like white fluid derived from the worker bees and usually fed to the larvae. The nurse bees in a honeybee colony produce royal jelly for five to fifteen days and feed the larvae for three days. If the honeybees want to raise a new queen, the specific larvae are fed royal jelly throughout its lifetime (from larvae to adult bee queen).

Human beings can also eat royal jelly as it is ideal for stimulating cell growth, great for neurological function, and has other health benefits. The beekeeper will need special equipment to harvest the royal jelly and can only get small substances at a time.

Propolis

A major component of propolis is the resins collected by bees, and it is harvested because it has antiseptic and detoxifying properties. Propolis has a lot of healing properties used to treat numerous health challenges such as diabetes, cold sores, colds, burns, and acne. The bees use propolis to build their hives by sealing spaces, cracks, and openings they don't want. Propolis also prevents microbial growth inside the hive.

Some of The Challenges Associated with Beekeeping

Start-up costs

When you start operating your beehive, you will realize that beekeeping is not expensive. Most costs are incurred at the start-up phase. You will need bee supplies, which include a hive, smoker, extracting equipment, and, of course, bees!

However, after buying these initial supplies, you may not have to buy more afterward (only tools for maintenance), which wouldn't cost you so much money.

Harmful bee stings

Bee stings are dangerous, and as a beekeeper, you and those around the beehive are most susceptible to these injuries. Do NOT keep bees if you or someone close to you is allergic to bees. If you are not allergic to bees, you will still have to be careful as bee stings hurt, and although you may develop immunity to the bees' poison, it is better to avoid it altogether.

Heavy lifting

Heavy lifting is involved during beekeeping as you will need boxes of frames used for honey production, which can weigh up to thirty to seventy pounds. These box frames will be lifted out of the hive to remove the honey and depending on the number of bees you have and how you are producing bee products, you will need to do some solid manual labor regularly.

Bee mess

As the bees fly around the hive, as they move from the hive to their food source and back, they will defecate, which leads to stains and unpleasant spots on the ground. They can also defecate on cars, outdoor furniture, and windows: if your beehive is not close to your home, then you wouldn't have to worry about this challenge as you only have to focus on cleaning inside the hive itself. But, if the beehive is close to your home, there will be more cases of bee mess.

The first-year blues

Another challenge of beekeeping is that in the first year, you won't get any honey, and this period is often referred to as the "First-year blues." At this time, you are just starting out, and so are the bees. You may not harvest anything in this first year as this is the time when bees need to keep the honey they make to provide their colony with enough food.

It is crucial to leave honey so bees can create their food: they have to gather nectar to make honey because they will need it for a good supply of food. If you take away that food, they make in the first year, they may not survive to give you more honey. A good beekeeper will have to ensure that the bees have enough honey to keep them through winter when there will be no food. This situation is challenging for beekeepers who are not patient enough in the first year. Please be patient in the first year.

The Advantages of Beekeeping

Locally made organic honey

Honey made from bees in your beehive is 100% organic and has many health benefits. Honey is a natural sweetener; it is full of nutrients such as pantothenic acid, iron, copper, calcium, manganese, phosphorus, and zinc. The honey derived from your beehive doesn't spoil, and it can be used in varying ways.

Honey can soothe coughs, it boosts memory, treats wounds, and prevents low white blood cell count. People who go through chemotherapy, experience low white blood cell count, and when they consume honey, it boosts their immune system to prevent such loss. Honey also relieves seasonal allergies, kills antibiotic-resistant bacteria, and provides fuel for the body. You can resolve lots of skin issues and scalp problems with honey.

Now with all these benefits honey brings, can you see how useful it is for you to own your beehive? You wouldn't have to buy honey and wonder if it is organic, and you will also have access to honey whenever you want it, as opposed to dealing with periodic honey scarcity.

Bee wax

Wax is a product of bees that can be used to make candles, body creams, lipsticks, lip balm, and cosmetics. During harvest time, beekeepers can collect wax and sell it to companies that use the product. If you are not engaging in beekeeping for commercial purposes, then you can use the wax.

Pollination

Bees help other plants remain healthy through pollination. The plants include fruit trees near the beehives, which is profitable for the local economy. If you situate your hives close to a garden, it is sure to bloom because of the impact of bees. If you want to enjoy this advantage as a beekeeper, then you should plant a garden close to your hive.

Low maintenance

Bees are very hard-working creatures, and, as such, little effort is required from you (well, aside from the initial set-up process). After starting your hive, when it begins operations, you will need about 30 minutes weekly for maintenance. Nor will you need much time to collect the honey (this will be about twice a year).

Unlike some other animals, bees are highly organized creatures with a sense of purpose. They stick together, and in most cases (if you take good care of them), they can ward off predators.

A fulfilling experience

Being a part of nature through beekeeping is a rewarding and fulfilling experience. You will observe the bees as infants grow into adults and watch them become beneficial to themselves and the flowers around them. Most beekeepers who take on this challenge for personal reasons agree that the joy of watching the bees flourish is worth the process.

You will also get closer to nature as you watch bees pollinate flowers and plants and see how they produce honey. The whole experience can be very soothing to the soul and provide you with a way of bonding with the natural world.

Bee conservation

When you become a beekeeper, you contribute to bee conservation efforts, which greatly benefit the species. When you become a part of conservation, you will enable periodic bee swarming, which will allow the restoration of the wild bee population. This wild population helps in sustaining the genetic diversity of the bee species.

Genetic diversity is a crucial step to enhance conservation efforts because bees have lately experienced a decline in population. Reversing this trend mostly appeals to people who are passionate about nature and strive to do their best with the conservation of animals. You can protect the bee habitat and nurture the ones that will create the next generation of bees, thus maintaining their life cycle.

Commercial gains (If desired)

Another benefit of beekeeping is the business gains; if you groom your bees well enough, they can give excellent yield during harvest so that you have enough to make a good sale. However, not everyone is interested in beekeeping for commercial purposes, so if you are, this will be a viable and long-term advantage. The value of honey and other products remains high across the world because of the shortage of bees.

Significant Factors to Consider in Beekeeping

The types of beehives

Where you keep the bees are crucial to the success of the entire process, and this location is referred to as "Apiary" or "bee yard." You must ask your local authorities about regulations concerning beekeeping (the rules vary from state to state).

If you want to grow bees in your backyard, then carry out a consultation with your neighbors to pre-inform them of your plans. This will avoid any future conflicts of interest. Next, you must consider the type of beehive to use, and while there are several types of beehives, there are some recommendations from experts.

British Standard national beehive

This beehive is standard in the United Kingdom; it is an affordable platform that makes it easier for the bees to assemble. This beehive offers a very efficient way of managing the bees as most beekeepers who have used it, do not complain about the bees; they only advise that beekeepers use a bigger brood box with this beehive.

Warre Hive

This type of beehive is easy to manage and ideal for those who are busy with other activities while maintaining the hive. If you can't spend a lot of time with the bees, then this hive is your best option.

Top bar beehive

The ease of using this beehive is one of the reasons beekeepers most prefer it as it can be constructed in record time and is very affordable. This beehive has a top-bar so that the bees are not disturbed during the inspection. This guarantees better quality honey production.

However, you should know that due to its top-bar design, this beehive may encourage bees to make more bee wax than honey. After every inspection, bees also need to build new combs, and this open bar design exposes the new combs to unfavorable weather conditions.

The Langstroth beehive

This beehive is a historic beehive that has been on the scene for about a century and a half: hobbyists and commercial beekeepers usually prefer it. The advantages of this beehive are numerous; hence, the reason it is popular is that it can be easily maintained and has a simple design with sufficient space for the bees.

This beehive also has chambers and frames that can be removed during the inspection and aids the proper division of bees. The colony can also be reused, but its disadvantage is that bees are disturbed during the inspection.

The site of the beehive

The best location for a colony is a sunny place (it should be a little bit shaded as well) with a water source close by. The hive should be placed so that it faces the south with a fence in the north that acts as a windbreak.

A field of flowers nearby is ideal for a beehive because this will make it easy for the bees to collect nectar and quickly get back to the hive. Before building the hive, check for possible predators and ascertain the extent of damage they could cause to your colony. Now, you don't want to invest in a beehive and lose your bees to predators, do you?

Access to supplies and tools

Another factor to consider is easy access to supplies and tools needed to keep the beehive safe and functional. When deciding on a location for your beehive, consider the proximity of the site to places where you can easily buy the things you need for the maintenance of your colony.

A commitment to consistency

Lastly, when planning a beekeeping venture, you must develop a commitment to the project. Unlike other rearing opportunities, bees require a lot of time. Commitment is crucial. Some beekeepers who easily give up on the project didn't consider the extent of involvement required before taking the first step.

This is the reason why I am talking about commitment from the start is to prepare you mentally for the journey ahead. However, you should know that despite the commitment level of this process, it is the most rewarding experience. Watching your bees grow and start producing honey while taking care of them is a wonderfully satisfying feeling, and when you start getting the rewards of your commitment, you will be proud of yourself.

The first chapter is complete! Well done, this was a general introductory chapter that provides insight into the nature of beekeeping and how you can harness this process for future gains. Due to the increase in demand for honey and other bee-derived products, there has been an increase in adulterated and fake bee products.

If you use honey a lot or if you use other bee products, you might want to consider grooming your bees to get organic products in real-time. Moving on from this chapter, I will be discussing more practical sections going forward as you start constructing your beehives.

*Most of the ideas, such as the site of your beehive and other basic concepts shared here will be comprehensively discussed in subsequent chapters.

Chapter Two:
Preparing Your Hive

From the first introductory section, we are moving on now to more practical aspects of how you can build your colony. In this chapter, you will find different steps to take in building your beehive or bee boxes. While there are multiple ways to get this done, I will stick to the most manageable steps with the most accessible materials that will make the process as seamless as possible.

Please note that not all aspects of the box will be built; some will have to be purchased (they may be too technical for you to make). As you read on, you will discover what you will construct and what you will buy.

Additionally, there are already made to fit bee boxes called "Bee kits," which come in the right dimensions. You can buy these or decide to build yourself, and if you are going to construct, then this chapter is for you.

Have you got your hammer and work apron? Let's build!

Step one: Choose a site for your bee box

The first step to take when preparing your hive is to know the location, area, and environment where the beehive will be located. Bees are adaptable and can stay in a wide variety of locations.

Regardless of where you are right now, you can usually find a good place for your beehive.

However, you will want a functional beehive, so the place you chose should be easily accessible, especially when it is time to collect the colony's honey. It is also helpful to have some space behind the hive, so you will have the freedom to work without bothering the bees as they enter and exit the hive.

Areas prone to flooding and high winds are not suitable for bee colonies. Both elements are dangerous to bees. Your hive should be situated on firm land that is not susceptible to flooding because excessive water can cause the hive to sink. If it is possible, please position your beehive close to wind blocks (trees or solid shrubs). Building your own wind guard is also a good idea.

Although a hive needs to be safe from the winds, you also want to avoid putting it in a location that's too shady because bees require warm temperatures inside their hive to be comfortable. Sunlight is helpful, and it will be nice if the bee box faces the direction of the sun (especially sunrise in the morning), so the bees can get warm early in the day.

The ground below your beehive should be leveled as well: if the field is not leveled, put some wood and stones under the hive so as to provide a solid foundation. This move will make it simpler for you to work around the bee box while the bees stay stable inside.

Of course, you have to choose a location that gives you access to necessary resources so that the colony can thrive. Choose a place with clean water and nectar-rich plants as these will help worker bees to stay refreshed.

Step two: Read and reread the plans (understand what you must do)

Next, you should read and reexamine the plans for the beehive by getting to know how you are going to set up and the process it entails. Unless you are getting someone else to do this for you, you must know what you are doing.

Step three: Check the materials and shopping list

What kind of tools will you need for the beehive? Get to know your shopping list (you will have one after reading this chapter), and when shopping for the materials, use your shopping list!

Step four: Understand the parts of the box

When you know the parts of your box, construction will be easier, and this entails:

- **The hive stand**

The hive stand lifts the hive off the ground, and it should have an angled landing board for the bees. You may not need a "Technical hive stand," but you will need a stand that props your super off the ground. You can use a bench or a balanced table that fits the honey box.

- **Bottom board**

The bottom board is the first layer of your box: it is a flat piece of wood, which is the base for the super. The bottom board can be solid or screened, the difference between both is that the screened bottom boards are great at keeping pests out while providing added ventilation. Your bees can come and go from the bottom board entrance.

- **The entrance reducer**

This part is a small piece of wood which blocks off part of the entrance at the bottom board. This part helps small bee colonies by making it difficult for large pests and predators to get in.

- **Slatted rack**

This part of your bee box is just as it sounds: slatted. It is a flat wooden panel crossed by other small strips of wood to form a flat rack. This part is also layered between the bottom board and the brood chamber, which provides ventilation for the bees. This part also allows access to the brood chamber, thus preventing the bees from forming "Ladder combs." Please note that the slatted rack is an optional addition to the box, but it is a great addition (if you use it).

- **Deep super**

The deep super is a bigger box where the bees build their hive, and this is also the most extensive section of the bee box (you will use one to two for one honeybee box) One deep super comes with about 8-10 frames.

- **Deep super-frames**

The deep super frames are inserted individually into the deep super as they hold the foundation. The latter is a wax and wire base the bees use to make their wax building. For this part, you will need eight to ten deep super frames (this will depend on the size of your deep super).

- **Queen excluder**

This part is essential because you don't want the queen bee to lay eggs inside the honey hence the reason it is added to the box. This part is a flat rack with small holes for the worker bees, but it is too small for the queen to use.

- **Honey super**

Honey super, just like the deep super, is the part of the box where the bees store their honey. This super is a large box put on top of the deep super with the queen excluder between them. It is better to work with shallow or medium-sized honey supers, as this will make it easy for you to lift the box when it is full of honey.

- **Honey super-frames**

The honey super-frames are panels made of either wood or plastic and inserted into the honey super vertically. These frames are where bees build their wax and honey; they can be removed from the super as well. The frames can either be shallow or medium to suit the size of the honey super you use and should have a foundation similar to the one in the deep super frames.

- **The inner cover**

The inner cover is the last layer of the bee box, which is a form of the lid that has an entrance placed over the honey super. The inner covers have two sides for the four seasons: one for fall/winter and one for spring/summer.

- **The outer cover**

The outer cover is a metal lid used to keep the bee box safe from adverse weather conditions. This part is also the lid that tops off the box above the top of the inner cover.

Step five: Build the bee box

After knowing your parts and the areas to note you are ready to build:

- **Purchase supplies**

When you are ready to build, the first step to take is to purchase your supplies, and you've got three choices when shopping for honeybee boxes. The first is to buy a complete box which will cost you more money. The second is to buy separate parts and assemble them, which will cost less than when you buy the whole box. The third is building all the pieces from scratch, which will save you over 50% of your money.

Irrespective of the option you choose, always purchase your supplies from a verified and authentic bee seller. It is not all about buying cheap supplies; you've got to ensure that your supplies are genuine so that they will last for a longer time. Use untreated wood (pine or cedar), and if the boxes don't have bottoms, you will have to purchase enough wood to create the outer parts for the different supers.

Some supplies, such as the outer lid or frames, have complicated construction processes; as such, you may have to purchase them.

Build the deep supers

The deep supers should have two short sides, which are 16.25-by-9.56 inches (41.28-by-24.28 cm). This part should also have two long sides of 20-by-9.56 inches (50.8-by-24.28cm). The four sides should have tongue-and-groove or dovetailed ends. Cut the wood to meet the measurements and create the joints at the edges.

Build the honey supers

The honey supers will vary in size depending on if you want them shallow or medium. However, the honey supers' length and width should be the same as the deep supers, with a long-side height of 6.625 inches. The small part by height should be 5.75 or 6.625inches.

The height of the honey supers may vary, but for a shallow super, the box should be five ¾ inches high while a medium super will be 6 5/8 inches tall. More so, just like the deep super, utilize tongue-and-groove or dovetailed joints on the edges.

Assemble the supers

Place the supers together using a small dab of glue on the interlocking joints with the help of waterproof glue. Then slide the slats into place to form your boxes; use a vice system to hold the boxes in place until the glue dries. After the glue dries, use small nails to complete the building process for the supers.

Build the bottom board (you can buy this)

The bottom board is the first layer of the box: it is a flat piece of wood that has raised edges.

The board should have the same length/width as the supers but with the sides (about 375-inches high). The entrance reducer should be attached to the front; it should be 75 inches, 1.91cm (for the summer entrance), and 95cm (the winter entrance).

A more massive entrance may accommodate rodents; make sure it fits. If you are unsure, then buy a base: most of them are reversible and made to fit. You will be saving costs of setup when you buy.

Paint the exposed parts of the box

You don't have to paint the box, but some beekeepers prefer to paint the exposed parts. They decorate it with white paint so it can reflect sunlight, and if you choose to do so, use non-toxic outdoor paint to withstand the weather. Do not paint inside the supers (it can be harmful to the honey and bees).

Buy the excluder

The excluder fits the top, which is inside the deep super and prevents the queen bee from moving into the honey supers. This excluder cannot be made at home, so you will have to purchase one for your box.

Buy the covers

You will need two covers for the honey box: the inner cover and the outer cover. The inner cover is wooden with a hole at the top (this serves as the entrance). The outer covering made of metal covers the top of the box. But the outer cover should contract over the sides of the hive, so it fits perfectly.

Get frames for the supers.

The frames refer to the portions of the box used by the bees to form the hive and wax. It might be a bit difficult to make your frames, and if you don't want to go through the process, you can purchase them. Frames are mostly made out of wood and plastic (they serve the same purpose).

For each deep super, you will need ten frames and 6-8 depending on the size of the honey supers. Now slide the frames into each super vertically until they are all in place.

Assemble the box

Now you can assemble your hive by putting the box together. You will need to layer all the parts on top of the stand with the bottom board going first. The slatted frame should be next and then the deep supers, followed by the queen excluder, honey super, and cover.

The hive stand will keep the beehive firmly off the ground with the bottom dry so that the bees are insulated. The hive stand can be constructed with any stable material (or you can buy one).

The beehive should be built days before the bees arrive as this will give time to paint it and allow the paint to dry up. Wet paint is not safe for bees, and it will make it even more difficult for them to settle into their new home. You also read the terms "Supers" a lot here: the wooden boxes that hold the comb's frames. The standard measurement for supers is 50.7 cm for the external length and 41.8cm for the width.

Although wood glue is crucial for a well-assembled beehive, if you are unable to get it during construction, you can still assemble the box without it. For nails, you should use box nails that are 50 mm or 1 1/8 inches, as these are ideal for nailing supers. You can also use flat-headed screws if you want the boxes to last longer. Some commercial beekeepers also use air-powered staple guns.

The paint you use should be one with a protective coating for the exteriors, as this will extend the life of the woodenware. Use house paint suitable for surfaces and do not use varnish interior paints as they are not long-lasting.

With this design, you can easily collect pollen using a pollen trap as the box is designed to trap pollen when the honeybee gets inside. A metal box is NOT recommended because of humidity levels. Wooden boxes allow the bees to breathe; they also absorb and expel moisture and try to match the humidity outside. If you use metal, it will trap the moisture and kill the bees.

When it comes to the wood of choice, I would advise that you do not use plywood because they contain toxic formaldehyde-based resins. If this substance comes in contact with the honey, it will contaminate it. Go for either cypress or cedarwood. The boxes should be at least 2 feet long and 3 feet tall with the wood 2 inches thick.

From the content of this chapter, you can tell that most of the work to be a beekeeper happens at the beginning stages. After setting up the hive, you will engage in less complex tasks. You've got your bee box and are ready to start the beekeeping process, so what should you do next? The next step to take entails getting your bees, which I will discuss in Chapter Three.

Chapter Three:
Introducing the Bees to The Hive

You have succeeded in building your bee box, and now your bees have a place to stay. As a new beekeeper, you will be excited at the prospects of bringing the bees into the bee box, but it is not enough to get the bees and put them inside. There are steps and factors to consider when doing this. In this chapter, you will learn these steps and additional information on the kind of bees to get as a beginner.

First, you have to learn where to buy the bees, how to reach honeybee sellers, various factors to consider when purchasing the bees, and then, of course, how to introduce the bees to their new home. This section is also a practical and comprehensive one; you will enjoy getting the bees.

Where do I buy bees?

Local beekeepers' association

Within different localities, various beekeeping associations handle bee-related issues. Most of these associations promote beekeeping amongst their members and engage in bee-related, economically driven activities. They ensure that bees are sold at a uniform price, maintain a standard with bee health, and if you find one such association, you can buy bees from them.

When you buy from such bee associations, you will enjoy some benefits which include:

- Learning about local bee guidelines
- Local bee laws and regulations
- Laws regarding their treatment.
- The economic viability of bees
- How to care for bees (especially as a beginner)
- How to feed them and information on where to get the best food
- You will also meet other beekeepers and learn from their experiences

Buying from another beekeeper

People keep bees for different reasons: some keep them for crop pollination, others see them as a hobby, and some others keep them to get honey. You can decide to buy your first bees from a beekeeper who keeps bees for sale as this seller would have nurtured the bees well enough to meet the sale standard. Also, buying bees from your locality is a better option than importing them.

When buying bees from a beekeeper, make sure the colony you purchase is free from disease, parasites, and pests. Check for mites and hive beetles as you certainly don't want these to be bothering your new colony: the losses you will incur from the impact of such pests will delay your entry into the beekeeping sector.

Buying packaged bees

The packaged bees come in a box with a queen bee. This kind of bee source can be delivered by mail, which is a popular choice in the USA. Many beginner beekeepers use these methods to start off. A typical package has bees in a box with screens on the side and the queen bee in a cage. You will also receive bee feeds inside the container.

When you receive your package, install the hive; do this in late afternoon or in the evening so the bees can enter the hive without flying around. Then free the queen bee from the cage; when you do this, the colony will accept the hive with ease.

However, you must be careful with packaged bees because some sellers are not genuine. If you must go with this option, ensure that you check the seller's reputation, get proper consultation, and ask the right questions before purchasing. Make sure the package is free from mites, honeybee diseases, and beetles.

Nuc hive bees

Another great way of getting bees is through a small nucleus hive, which has a few frames of bee brood and honey. This hive comes with a queen and several thousand bees as most honeybee sellers will have this option readily available for sale. The nuc box is usually bought in springtime and placed inside a standard beehive box.

The bees in the nuc box will expand into the beehive box, and the nuc box can then be taken out later. Nucleus hives are an excellent way to kick-start your bee colony. Honey included in this hive is also advantageous to the bees as it will be their initial food before they start rummaging for nectar and getting pollen.

Another advantage of the nuc hive is that it is an excellent way of starting a new bee colony quickly: it comes with a working colony of honeybees. With this method, the bees don't need time to get used to each other. They also do not need time to get used to the queen bee: frames and combs in this hive are already drawn.

How can I reach honeybee sellers?

There are varying ways of reaching honeybee sellers. You can buy from local sellers in your area or from the beekeepers' association (a face-to-face meeting is advised so you can inspect the bees yourself). You can also talk to the sellers online or via telephone.

However, if you cannot have a face-to-face meeting, you must do due diligence to ensure that the supplier is genuine. You can find some great bee sellers listed in newspapers and ads; ask your friends and fellow beekeepers who may have bought from some bee sellers.

The internet is replete with resources on how you can find suitable bee suppliers in your locality. However, do not rely on your findings online, always do a background check on all suppliers, and if you are still unsure, you can start by buying in small batches.

What Are the Factors to Consider When Buying Bees?

Work with a genuine bee seller

Check the credentials of the bee seller before purchasing. Choosing an excellent seller with experience in handling bees will guarantee a productive beekeeping experience. It would help if you had a bee seller who is excellent at nurturing, packaging, and shipping bees, and you can get this information through online reviews and asking previous clients.

Do not buy bees from suppliers with negative reviews who do not fulfill their promises to beekeepers. Also, do not buy from those with poor handling services as this will make the bees vulnerable to pests and diseases.

Buy bees in established colonies from a local beekeeper

You very likely already know that bees are social insects that live together in a single colony. Their survival depends on each other's safety: if you buy bees, then getting an established colony will make it easier for the bees to multiply very fast and aid their survival.

Buy at least two colonies and put them in different hives. This double placement will help you still have access to the right hive if one becomes weaker.

When you buy bees for a starter colony (especially from beekeepers), ask if they can sell the bees in "Nuc hives" as this helps you get a better bee colony with healthy bees.

Always check shipment boxes to ensure they are safe from mites

Before putting the bees into the hive, ascertain if they are free from bugs or ants because these are predators that feed on honey and the larvae of bees. If bugs and ants are allowed to feed on the honey, it can force the entire colony to change location.

Beekeepers with bee colonies that are infested by mites, ants, beetles, and other diseases should not sell bees. Also, for everyone's safety, only honey from healthy and safe colonies should be sold.

A lot of regions have rules regarding the sale and importation of honeybees; if an area is free from varroa mites, it would be wrong to bring in bees from mite-infested colonies. You can use pest control in such situations, but it is better to avoid the problem from the start.

Buy bees in nucleus or starter hives

A nucleus consists of worker bees, the queen bee, and may take about 4-5 frames. This type will ensure that the colony is complete with a queen, workers, and drone, which will make your hive a good one. As opposed to packaged bees, the nucleus has a far greater chance at survival in any beehive.

Things to Note Before Buying the Bees

Getting the honeybee colony is the next step in your beekeeping process, and some of the things to note are:

Research different types of bees

Before getting your bees, you've got to read about the kinds of bees you can use as a beginner beekeeper. Bees vary in temperament, resistance to disease, foraging power, parasite and pest control. However, getting the bees in your locality will be helpful as it will make adaptability easier for them, but this doesn't mean that all kinds of local bees are great for you. Find out the best kind of bees for your peculiar environment by carrying out research and asking other beekeepers in your locality.

Get your housing ready

I talked about the beehive itself in the previous chapter, so make a last inspection to ensure it is fit for the bees. Consider if the bee box is easy to use, and can it expand? Does it have the capacity to keep the bees safe in winter? You can also consider having some replacement parts of the hive close by just in case something goes wrong.

Get beekeeping equipment

Beekeeping equipment should be nearby as you prepare to get the bees inside. Beekeeping is also more about the management of bees; you will need the requisite tools to ensure proper management, and some of these tools include hive tools, bee feeders, hive beetle traps, and mite treatments. You can also get parasite treatments (you will learn more about pest control in a beehive in Chapter Seven).

Feeding the installed colony of honeybees

Before getting your bees to the hive, you should get some bee food. In Chapter Four, I will discuss extensively the subject of feeding bees and the kind of foods you should get, but before then, let's explore the concept briefly.

Pollen patties and sugar are some of the significant sources of feeds for bees: the sugar is dissolved in water and the pollen patties given in their original state to the bees. You can also purchase these bee feeds ahead of time and stock up on a lot of them until the bees start to create their food. A well-fed bee colony will settle into the hive faster, become more robust, and will produce high-quality honey.

A beehive location

Location is everything with your beekeeping activities, as it is a major determining factor that will decide the kind of yields you get from the bees. Consider proximity to your home and a safe place, so the bees don't sting people: please avoid footpaths and areas with a lot of human traffic as these are not ideal sites.

Be compliant with local laws and regulation governing beekeeping

Again, different states and countries have specific legislation regarding beekeeping, and it is your responsibility to know these laws. Ensure you are not breaking any of the statutes as compliance will help you avoid issues that will lead to the shutdown of your beekeeping operations.

Can I Catch Bees Instead of Buying Them?

You can catch a swarm of bees and install them in a beehive, especially if you don't want to buy bees. Occasionally a honeybee colony will split into two or more swarms, and this split will lead to the establishment of new colonies. When this happens, beekeepers can catch the swarms and use them in their bee boxes as honeybee colonies.

Beekeepers love wild swarms because of the kind of genetic variance they bring to the bee boxes. But these variations also bring some unwanted characteristics to the genetic pool of honey in your box (this will affect the temperament of the hive).

Getting the swarm of bees is not always easy, as even experienced beekeepers struggle with it sometimes. You may set traps to catch the swarm of bees and get a swarm immediately, but in some cases, you may never get anything. This process makes finding a swarm unreliable because it is unpredictable; this should be something you do much later and not as a beginner.

When you become experienced as a beekeeper, you can use specially prepared trap boxes that mimic the trees. The hollows are supposed to be of a specific minimum volume and size to attract the swarming bees, but it shouldn't be too heavy to handle when they catch a swarm.

Steps on How to Place Your Bees in A Hive

Before placing your bees in the colony, make sure you've got these tools: the hive stand, bottom board, one hive body, ten frames (for a ten-frame hive), inner cover, entrance cover, and feeder.

Step one

Get the bees as soon as they arrive, check if they are still alive (if there are dead bees piled up at the bottom, then there's a problem, please call the supplier). Then, install the bees as soon as possible; if you want to wait for a day or two, then put the bees in a cool place (not a cold place). It should be a dark area like a garage or a basement and keep a close eye on them. But if you can install the bees immediately, please do! That would be, by far, the best approach.

Then, you will need a hive tool, lit smoker, smoker fuel and lighter, a bee brush, a bee suit, pocketknife, duct tape, and rubber bands.

Step two

Now you can install the bees by late afternoon by first ensuring the smoker is well-lit. Although the smoker is not usually used for installing packaged bees, it is good to get into the habit when you start inspecting your hives. Open the lid of the place where you have the bees (depending on how you got them), remove the feeder jar, and hold the tab for the queen cage. Remove the queen cage from the other bees and replace the lid, so the bees do not escape. Open your hive and remove 3-4 frames from one side; if the bees cluster on the queen cage, brush them off so you can inspect the queen.

Step three

Inspect the queen to make sure she is alive and healthy, watch her walk, and check that she is not gimpy. If you can, count her legs to be sure they're complete, and if you find that the queen is dead, injured, or looking unhealthy, then put her back in the cage and return the bees to the seller. If the queen is healthy, then go ahead and place her in the hive.

Step four

To place the queen in the hive, you can use three methods:

The rubber band method entails placing a rubber band around one frame in the hive and putting the queen's cage between the band and the foundation. You can install the cage vertically just behind the rubber band.

Then, replace the frame with the queen cage at the center of the hive (the queen should always be at the center) then place another frame next to the queen's cage.

You can use the rim board method, which entails placing the queen cage on top of the frames facing up and putting the rim board around her. After removing the cork from the queen's cage, lay the cage on the top bars to be at the center of the hive. Then, place the rim board on the hive to allow the bees some space to cluster around the queen.

Another method requires you to use a drawn comb to push the queen's cage into the wax, thus sticking it to the comb. This method is excellent when it is warm outside. Ensure the candy end of the hive is accessible: after the queen's cage is secure, place another frame against the frame with the enclosure. After installing the queen bee, you can then install the bees.

Step five

Shake a few bees on top of the queen; the bees will stick their butts in the air and release "Nasonov pheromone," which informs the other bees that the queen is present. Shake the bees into the hive where you got the frames from (try to get as many bees in as you can). Now don't worry if you don't get all the bees out; the rest of the bees will surely find their way to the hive.

Next, replace the frames but don't push them in or crush the bees from the top: allow them to fall into place gently. If you used the rim board method, first place the rim board on the hive, put the inner cover before the outer cover. Brush the bee out of the way when replacing the covers. Leave the container or package you used to get the bees close to the hive, so bees left out in the transfer process can find the colony.

Step six

Although I will talk about feeding in detail in the next chapter, you should know about the first feeding stages right after installing the bees. You can use a feeder to give them honey, beebread, or pollen, so they don't starve, and you will have to feed them until they can make their food, wax, and build a home inside the hive.

Always keep the feeder full, and you can also feed the bees 1:1 syrup (your local bee store will know this) until they are on all ten frames. Don't overfeed them, though.

Step seven

After installing your bee package, do not touch the hive for a week as you might disturb them, which will make them kill the queen instead of accepting her. Keep the feeder full; the bees will fly around (this is okay; they are a bit confused right now), and soon, they will get used to their new environment.

Use this time to search for other bees carrying dead bees (these are called undertaker bees), and it is a sign that the colony is thriving. Also, look out for bees bringing in pollen (which is needed to feed in the hive); it is a good sign that the queen will lay soon.

Step eight

After one week, suit up and smoke the bees with a puff at the entrance and whiff under the cover. Open the hive and inspect the queen, check if she has been released from the cage. If she has been released, then it is time to remove the queen cage, and if she hasn't, confirm if she is still alive. Remove the cork from the candy end, and be careful not to allow the queen to fly away. Then, put the cage back in, close the hive and recheck it in a few days. After a few days, check the hive for eggs and make sure the queen has started laying.

How To Identify The Queen Bee

Throughout this chapter, I have mentioned the queen bee, and you may be wondering, "How can I tell which is the queen bee?" Well, if you got your bees from a packaged service or directly from a seller, they may separate the queen bee for you, but if you got your bees through a different means, you might have difficulty identifying her.

1. The queen bee is the colony leader and the mother of most of the bees (worker and drone bees). If the queen is healthy, the hive will thrive and vice versa. When she grows old and dies, the hive will die if it doesn't get a new queen. As such, to maintain your hive, you

must distinguish the queen from the other bees, and the steps below will help you.
2. Look for the largest bee: the queen bee is longer and narrower.
3. All honeybees have a blunt abdomen, but the belly of a queen bee is pointed (you can tell her apart from the others this way).
4. Queens are also much more visible because they sit with their legs spread while other bees have their legs under their bodies.
5. Only one queen lives in a hive, and if you find more than one bee with the above characteristics, then lift it to inspect the middle part of its body. You can use a magnifying glass here; the queen will be one with smooth and un-barbed stingers.
6. You can locate the queen by gently removing each of the hive frames and look for the larvae. The queen will be close by because she lays all the eggs. However, be careful when doing this so that you don't injure or kill the queen.
7. You can also spot the queen through movement. Worker and drone bees will always move away from her path, and they cluster together where she is as well.

The rest of the hive takes care of the queen, so you can spot her easily by looking for the bee that isn't doing anything but just eating.

After identifying her, mark her by coloring her, and there is a beekeeper's way of doing this. Beekeepers use specific colors to identify the queen based on how many years the queen has left to live. By marking the queen, you will know when you need a new queen soon, and you can protect the hive before the queen dies.

If the queen has between 1-6 years to the end of her reign, use white paint on her thorax. If she has 2-7 years of her reign, use yellow paint. Use red color for 3-8 years, use green color, for 4-9 years, and for 5-10 years use blue paint. Be careful with removing her, marking her, and putting her back as you don't want to hurt her in the process.

As more people get into beekeeping, it may seem challenging to get access to healthy bees, depending on where you are. This realization is the reason why buying bees from local beekeepers' associations and local beekeepers is a great option. Buying from such sellers is better than importing bees, as locally bred bees can more quickly adapt to their local environment than those from abroad.

In conclusion, before placing the bees in the hive, please get approval from the local government and other beekeeping authorities within your locality. Now your bees are home; you need to start the process of nurturing and grooming them. Feeding is the first step to take: in the next section, you will learn more about how to *feed* and *nurture* bees.

Chapter Four:
Feeding and Nurturing Bees

This chapter focuses on two fundamental ideas about beekeeping: how to feed and nurture them. This covers the kind of food you should give the bees, when to provide them with such meals, and how to ensure they are not overfed. The nurturing section focuses on some steps you can take towards ensuring that your bees are 100% healthy and safe. Both ideas (feeding and nurturing) work together because when bees are well fed and in a suitable environment, they will thrive.

However, if you feed them well without taking care of the environment or other aspects of their welfare, they will not survive. So, let's learn how to achieve both ideas.

How to Nurture Bees

To become excellent at nurturing bees, you must first understand why bees are so important. Regardless of your reasons for becoming a beekeeper, you should know that bees are disappearing globally. Global warming, excessive use of pesticides, and habitat loss are some of the reasons for their disappearance.

Now some people who do not understand the impact of this loss may say, "So what?" and not bother about it. But the truth is that the dwindling bee population is disastrous for humankind. Did you know that more than one-third of all food crop production in the USA requires pollination?

That one-third encompasses many different types of crops, including some kinds of fruits, vegetables, and nuts. Bees are also primary pollinators that aid the increase of fruit and vegetables during harvest, and they add $15 billion to the economy of the United States yearly.

These facts and figures mean that without bees, you will never enjoy many of your favorite crops, which include plants like apples, blueberries, cherries, cranberries, limes, lemons, mangoes, plums, pumpkin, watermelon, etc.

As such, regardless of your reason for becoming a beekeeper (a hobby, economic reasons, or because you like it), by nurturing bees the best way you are contributing to stabilizing nature and helping in the achievement of environmental balance. You can contribute to the movement by ensuring that you nurture your bees well, and the steps below will help you:

- **Reduce the use of insecticides**

Insecticides are a massive problem to bees even though they are ostensibly used to help the bees stay safe from pests. Pesticides are toxic and contain harmful chemicals that can kill bees even when you think you are trying to keep them safe. Pesticides can wipe out an entire colony of bees and the honey (making it harmful for consumption). Even some "Biodegradable" pesticides are toxic, so instead of using them, many people try natural solutions such as praying mantises and homemade spray using onion, pepper, or garlic.

- **Don't be quick to weed**

If you love gardening, you will surely hate weeds, but don't be quick to get rid of them, especially when you are beekeeping. For example, dandelions and cloves are loved by bees, so keeping them will help the bees stay nourished. Now, this doesn't mean you shouldn't get rid of weeds at all: just get rid of some and leave some for the bees (you have some new friends to consider now, right?).

- **Select plants that bees love**

While bees pollinate lots of plants (they can visit the same plant repeatedly), there are particular plants they love. Bees like native wildflowers that can thrive in your climate; you can also get flowering herbs such as sage, rosemary, mint, and thyme with lavender as these are excellent pollinating choices for bees.

Plant these nearby, and you will be giving your bees a treat! You can also get sunflowers, coneflowers, daisies, and marigolds as these are fantastic options for bees. More so, single flowers are more easily accessible to bees than double ones, and you may want to have particular colors of plants together. When you have the same shade of plants together, it will make it easier for the bee to locate its favorite.

Here is a fun fact: blue and purple-colored flowers attract more bees, so remember this when planning your bee garden. Also, choose an array of blooms that will flower from spring till fall, as this will help provide good pollen throughout these seasons.

- **Get a water source**

Like other animals, bees need water to survive, and you can help them by getting a shallow water source where they can drink water. Fill the container with water and include some natural elements such as twigs and pebbles (they can rest on these as they drink water).

However, make sure you freshen the water daily so your bees know they can come every day and drink clean water. Yes, I know it is a lot of work, but if you are going to get the best out of the bees, you must put in the work.

- **Offer shelter and suitable habitat**

One of the reasons why bee stings happen a lot with some beekeepers is that the bees do not feel welcomed in their new home. They become restless, aggressive, and unable to produce good honey. However, your bees will be happy if you bring them into a comfortable space that feels like home.

This consideration is one of the reasons why I talked extensively on where to site your hive. If you place your hive in a dry place, with no access to water or in an area without flowers nearby, your bees will not be happy. If you have some muddy spots, soil, and untreated wood around to make them feel closer to nature they will be happier.

- **Proper cleaning and maintenance**

The fact that your bees look alright and everything seems fine doesn't mean you shouldn't clean the hive. Regular maintenance is crucial for the safety of the bees. You must check to ensure pests are not in the colony and that the bees are healthy. I will discuss the subject of pests and disease control in Chapter Seven.

But, before we get to that chapter, have a maintenance plan for your hive based on recommendations from the experts and experienced beekeepers. Don't wait until it is convenient for you to maintain and clean the hive before doing it.

- **Learn how to help a tired bee**

You can nurture your beehive by continually monitoring the bees, and if you see a bee struggling to fly, then know that it is injured or about to die. However, in some cases, the bee may just be tired. To help it regain its strength, mix two tablespoons of sugar and one teaspoon of water. Place the mix on a plate or a spoon and encourage the bee to drink it.

The mixture shouldn't have sweeteners or honey from your kitchen shelf, and you can leave the mix somewhere close by so the bee can get some. If you see a bee resting on a flower, it may not be weak; it may be resting, so keep a close eye. Remember that these are creatures, they cannot tell you when they are sick, but through constant monitoring and inspection, you can tell when things are not right.

- **Become a champion for bees**

Lastly, in your own little way, you can champion the bee's cause by educating more people about the impact of a decline on our economy and nature. Bee organizations in several localities have people who are passionate about bees for different reasons. If you join such organizations, you can lend your voice and contribute your quota to help bees stay alive.

Remember that if no one takes action, if you don't and I don't, then you wouldn't have bees to groom. If you join the beekeepers' association in your locality, use their platform to make more people understand why this is important. Again, this is not a pressure call to make you a "Bee activist," but it's certainly a worthwhile cause and something you should think about.

You can talk to your family members or friends. Some of them may not understand why you are interested in bees, so make them know why by sharing all you've learned about the impact of bees on nature and the economy.

Feeding Bees

Although allowing bees to gather their food is ideal, you should also know that you can create food for them if, for some reason, there are inadequate sources of honey in the environment. You can create their food if they are unable to make it themselves, especially within the first week of their stay in the hive. There are various types of feeders, sugar mixes, and times for feeding.

Step one: Chose a feeder

There are different types of feeders, and some of them include:

- **The frame feeder**

You can work with a frame feeder, a conventional feeder made of either wood or plastic. Your feeder should also be between the 1-2-gallon range and one with a coarse sliding feature that allows the bees to climb the sides. Also, get a feeder with floats to prevent the bees from drowning if water gets inside.

You can find these models in popular bee stores and make sure you have feeders that are easy to use (you can open them quickly to change feed and clean them easily as well).

- **The Boardman feeder**

If you don't want bees to drown, use the frame or miller feeders as wooden feeders that look like large boxes. These feeders can hold a mason jar with food upside down, just place it at the entrance, and the bees will get into the pot for the syrup. The containers are also easy to manage. However, to refill them, you may have to shake them gently.

- **The inverted feeder**

This feeder is like a watercooler that works like the inverted mason jars as you can place it at the top entrance, so the bees fly into it. You can cover the door with a cloth, so the bees don't hover around the jar when you have to refill it. With this feeder, your bees will face a lesser risk of drowning.

- **The miller feeder**

If you want to handle lots of bees, this model will work for you as it is a plywood feeder with a larger capacity than average feeders. The miller feeders give the bees open access, so they fly around the hive through the feeder, and with this feeder, you can hold more syrup. Remember to clean the feeders, replace spoilt food, and keep the bees safe.

Step two: Prepare to enter the feeder

To enter the feeder, you will purchase cotton suits for comfort, which will give you some freedom to move around and keep the bees away. Get a suit with leg zippers, knee pads, elastic wrists, gusseted crotch, and with a double-ended zipper. Your outfit should also have a pocket where you can put tools, and, obviously, it should be sting proof. The prices of such suits vary depending on their features and fabric quality, so please buy what you can afford.

Next, light the smoker using a cigarette lighter or match, but don't make it too hot. Puff one or two spurts of smoke at the entrance and the top of the feeder as this will disarm the bees' pheromones. Wait for a minute after the puffs before opening the hive, and if you see that the bees are still restless, use an extra puff. Also, follow the instruction manual of the smoker you use.

Step three: Mix the syrup

This syrup can be used if you don't have honey to feed the bees. It is easy to make, as you will only need sugar and water.

- 1 pound of sugar or 5 pounds of sugar

- 1 quart of water or 5 quarts of water

Stir the sugar into the warm water (use the measurement based on how much or how little you want to make). First, remove the water from the heat before adding the sugar, and after doing this, allow it cool before feeding the bees.

Step four: Schedule the feeding times

Lastly, you've got to set up a feeding schedule. Winter is usually the hardest time for bees, as some of them can't get food, so they starve. You must plan a feeding schedule that will help you feed your bees in winter. Prepare the feeding syrup recipes in August or September (you can also do it in October, but don't wait until December).

Please ask other local beekeepers if you don't know the amount of food to store for winter. Then use the seasonally mixed syrups to prepare gallons of food. Only give the hive additional feeds when they seem to need it, so you don't overfeed them.

Then, use your calendar to plan how you will feed them daily using the information you get from other experienced beekeepers, and your observation of your bees eating patterns.

Nurturing bees the right way with a sustainable goal in mind will help you not only achieve more with your bees. It also contributes to global conservation efforts. Now, you don't have to feel so much pressure just because I talked about conservation. I simply want you to know that your efforts matter, and you are doing more than grow bees.

The more you feed the bees and nurture them, the better you become at it, so it becomes a part of your routine. The first few weeks of beekeeping may be a bit challenging, especially if you have a busy schedule, but don't worry, as time goes on, you will get used to it. Now, let's learn all about bee seasons in Chapter Five!

Chapter Five:
Beekeeping Seasons

Beekeeping is not only about getting the hive, feeding them, and harvesting the honey. You also have to understand the seasons. There are beekeeping seasons that represent times when it is excellent to keep bees, and times when you have to be mindful of the process. Knowing how the seasons work is crucial to succeeding in this venture, and you are going to learn a lot about this subject here.

Spring is usually the ideal time to get bees, but as a beekeeper, your work will last through to late winter and late fall. There are, however, activities you can engage in throughout all the seasons. Below, I will analyze bee seasons and answer some vital questions about this topic. You will also learn what you can do each month (your work as beekeeper changes with each month). Let us begin from January 1: Late winter!

Seasonal Guide for Beekeeping

Late winter

During late winter, the bees are in a cluster for warmth, so cleaning happens on warm sunny days when they split from the groups. For some beekeepers, the year starts in late winter, so they try to ascertain how their bees made it through winter.

Check the bees' weight, feed them regularly, and clean out dead bees and debris from the bottom board for proper ventilation.

Early spring

As the days become warmer, the bees will fly around foraging for pollen and nectar. When the temperature gets to the 50's, carry out a full hive inspection by checking the brood and monitoring the queen. Check if the bees still have honey stores (stored pollen) and if the bottom box is empty.

If the bottom box is empty, then it means all the bees are at the top, so reverse the brood boxes by placing the top box at the bottom. If the weather is warm, feed the bees 1:1 sugar syrup (1 pound of sugar and 1 pint of water), and now is also the time to purchase more bees as your queen might be needing a successor.

Spring

In spring, the bees forage earnestly, and the queen will lay about 1-2,000 eggs daily (colonies will increase in population). If you want to start the beekeeping process, then now is the best time. If you have already begun, then treat the hive for mites and note that this is the season for swarms (because of the increase in population). Monitor the colonies closely and divide hives that show signs of swarming.

Early summer

In early summer, bee colonies increase in size, and this is the season when you should keep an eye on the colonies via weekly inspections. By now, you should be done feeding them, but you have to ensure the queen is laying well, and large colonies are not swarmed. At this time, you can combine weak hives with strong ones or split a robust territory into two if the bees are filling the chambers.

Summer

In summer, the hive is in full swing with bees foraging and producing lots of honey! Summertime is a period to enjoy the benefits of the beehive (if the weather is good). You will also enjoy simply watching the colony if there are lots of plants for bees to visit and delight in. Add some honey supers to the hive at this time. Check for mites every week and treat the hive, while keeping an eye on the queen to be sure she's healthy with a strong egg-laying pattern.

Also, look out for signs of swarming or robbing by yellow jacket and hornet bees (you can place a robbing screen over the entrances).

The Honey Harvesting Season

Some beekeepers start harvesting in August or early September, so you might want to take the honey supers, collect the frames after using the smoker to set the bees aside. Extract the honey (this should be on a warm day and in an enclosed space where the bees cannot get to). If you do it in an open space, the bees will stay stuck to the honey.

August shortage

In August, the bees may start eating their honey if there is a shortage, and this shortage is often known as the "Nectar Dearth."

The nectar dearth happens when flowers dry or are bloomless, leaving little nectar available for the bees to harvest.

So, if the bees eat the honey in their stores, you have to start feeding them again while keeping an eye on the weather. Also, find out if this summer shortage is a general and long-lasting phenomenon in your locality.

Fall

Bees store food during this period, and most beekeepers call this season the "Robbing season" as bees rob honey from weaker hives. Bees can steal honey from other colonies. You should give them a boost since they are still quite physically active at this point in the year. Give them 2:1 sugar syrup to prepare them for winter.

If you did not medicate the bees in August, then now is a good time to do that as mites tend to peak in October and September, and you will want your bees safe from bugs as they get into winter.

Late fall

In late fall, bees will stay in the hive more because the weather will be below 50 degrees. At this time, you should prepare for winter if moisture is a problem in your area, then use quilt boxes, and in some cases, you may have to combine weak hives. You should also clean the apiary during late fall, put mouse guards, and some insulating material around the hive. Use a scale to get an idea of the weight of your hive, as it will give insight into the amount of honey in the colony.

Winter in the hive

In the cold season, the bees will cluster in the colony, but the queen won't lay eggs. If the bees have foraged well for food and you fed them well during the fall season, there will be enough honey for them in winter. Check the weight of the hive occasionally: if it is lighter, you have to start feeding the bees again (solid sugar or sugar cakes). However, it will be better for the bees to feed on their winter food storage, but if they don't have enough food, you have to intervene and help them.

A Monthly Guide for Beekeeping

December, January, and February

During these winter months, monitor the hive carefully, especially the entrance for a buildup of dead bees. Also, inspect the structure for woodpecker or wind damage while making sure the roof stays secure. Use a strap, bricks, or blocks to keep the roof safe and also check for food weight. If the food on the feeder is light, then replace it and record all observations as you leave the winter months. During these months, you can also inspect the exterior of the hive, verify the hive tops are secure, and observe the bee entrances while monitoring the clusters.

During these months, you will need:

- Record book
- Protective clothing
- Straps
- Bricks

- Wedges
- Smoker
- Hive tools

March

In early March, monitor the hive's entrance for damages by weather or pest attacks and pay attention to its weight. If the weather is getting warm, then the bees will increase, which means their food consumption will also increase. During this month you will need:

- Protective clothing
- Smoker
- Hive tools
- Feeder and syrup
- Record book

April

By April, the bee colony will be multiplying, and food supplies must be maintained, and on a warm day, you can remove the entrance block. Then, change the floor to a clean one, remove the feeder, and replace the queen excluder with a super. Get rid of all honey flows into the supers and be vigilant for swarming as it can start in April. Also, watch for signs of spring disease, make sure to add frames, provide laying space, and clustering space. You should also include supers to give the storage space for nectar.

For this month you will need tools such as:

- Feeder and syrup
- Protective clothing
- Clean floor
- Sterilized extractor
- Rubbish bag
- Record book
- Bait hive

May

May is a good time for beekeeping, as you will observe large and more robust colonies with young ones growing fast and the hive's fragrance everywhere. However, it is not a time to become complacent; you have to carry out a more thorough inspection of the hive and the brood comb. Take the old bee combs outside to be removed and replaced as such old combs are disease-ridden and should be replaced. Remove the outer frames that are clogged with food and ensure the hive has enough food and pollen.

Put new frames and foundation on the side of the brood nest so the queen can increase her nest size: if it is too congested, it can lead to swarming. Additional supers may be needed at this time as well.

The tools you will use in May includes:

- Hive tools
- Record book
- Bait hives and swarm lures
- Rubbish disposal bag

- New frames (foundation and spare brood chamber)

June

In June, you are expected to examine the hive for possible changes, especially the brood frames for signs of disease or swarming. The brood will occupy most of the chamber this month, and swarming will continue throughout June, so be vigilant. You may take off some frames of capped honey or complete supers, but ensure you have empty frames or supers to replace the ones you take.

The hives in June are healthier, more energetic, and young colonies; thus, you should pay closer attention to them. In this month, you should evaluate stronger queens, ensure that the bees have enough water, and keep notes while inspecting the colonies.

Here you will need:

- Bee escapes for clearing the supers (bee brush)
- Spare supers, frames, and foundation
- New brood frames
- Protective clothing
- Smoker
- Hive tools
- Record book

July and August

Swarming will end by early July, thus allowing you and the colony to collect nectar. The honey to be harvested and the queen excluder should be taken off in early August, thus allowing the bees to collect some more remnants of food because, by early August, you will have to reduce the entrances so the colony can defend itself from wasps.

At this time you will need:

- Entrance blocks
- Record book
- Protective clothing
- Smoker
- Hive tools
- Bee brush
- Spare supers, frames, and foundation
- Bee escapes (for cleaning the supers)
- Varroa strips

September

In September, you have to feed the colony for winter and replace the honey you removed. Add 1kg bag of granulated sugar into a pint of water until the sugar dissolves, then add fumidil B for Nosema: the hive will need at least 15kg of this syrup, especially if it is a bigger hive. Feeding the bees should be completed before the end of the month, thus allowing the colony to get rid of excess water: remove the varroa strips after 42 days. Put the mouse guard at the entrance and get these tools:

- Record book
- Large bucket type feeders
- Protective clothing
- Smoker

- Hive tool

October, November, and December

Everything should be alright in winter because you have all the syrup in the hive. You can place a mouse guard at the entrance if you haven't done this, and then strap the roof against the winter wind. Always monitor the small entry occasionally for dead bees as some will die, but if you don't check, it might lead to the death of the entire colony.

Also, check for woodpecker damage, check for rain getting into the hive, and watch out for animals that may want to attack the colony at night. Feeding may not be required at this time; remember that the bees have gathered food for winter but always have an emergency block of candy. It's not unknown for colonies to die because of starvation in winter; make sure you have some food for them in an emergency.

Bees are, essentially, a kind of livestock. That means they need a regular checkup, and during this time, you will need:

- Candy blocks
- Mouse guards
- Straps
- Record book (write down all changes you observe)
- Protective clothing
- Hive tool
- Smoker

Questions on Bee Seasons

What time of the year should you get bees?

Usually, early spring, as this is when the queen lays eggs after the winter break. The colonies will build their population at this time. They will forage for nectar and pollen to store, and the precise date for all these to happen depends on the weather. You can purchase queen bees in summer and into fall as suppliers always sell out after spring: you may get nucs, swarms, and splits from beekeepers during summer.

When should you keep bees?

It is recommended to start the hive in spring as this will allow the bees to build and thrive in their colonies. They can also build food stores to protect them when winter comes. But, aside from keeping bees in the right season, you should take the overall step of starting a hive when you have learned all it takes to become a beekeeper, just as you are doing now.

There are many bee clubs, bee associations, suppliers, sellers, and online groups you can join to learn more practical aspects of beekeeping before embarking on your journey. If you can get a "Beekeeping mentor," then go right ahead: someone more experienced than you who will teach you how to get things right as a beginner. When you take these right steps, you will prepare yourself to manage the bees the best way: you will know when you are ready!

Which month should you harvest honey?

Traditionally, the month for harvest is in late summer and early fall. In some places, there is a consistent flow of nectar in plants that make desirable honey. The new honey supers will be placed in the hive, so the nectar is separated from other nectar flows, and the honey will be collected when the bees process it.

Bee types such as chestnut honey and Italian honey can be harvested in June and July. I will talk about the harvesting process in Chapter Six.

Where do the bees go in fall?

Bees stay in their hive in fall, which is different from birds and other insects that die in fall or winter. Bees go about their daily business of raising their brood and foraging for pollen and nectar. Fall is a busy period for them. They use the fall season to gather enough food to be stored for winter.

Can I start a beehive in the fall season?

You can start a beehive in the fall season, but you should know that the chances of the colony surviving through winter are slim. For a bee colony to set up a proper hive, they have to draw a comb, make honey, and get enough pollen for winter. It's hard for them to have enough time if you start in the fall. However, if you set it up in spring, by the time it gets to fall, the bees are stronger and used to their new hive.

What time of the year do bees swarm?

Bees swarm whenever they feel overcrowded in their hive, and most swarms happen in late spring to early summer. You will find fewer hordes in summer, and some outlier swarms may occur in the fall season.

What temperature is too cold for the hive?

Bees can handle the freezing winter as they tend to cluster in a ball in the hive and generate heat to maintain their temperature by up to 95 degrees. The bees will keep the queen in the middle of the cluster to protect her.

But, for the rest of the period, they don't fly unless the temperature gets to 50 degrees. If the temperature is lower than 50 degrees, the bees will be too cold to fly back to the hive. So, even though they can handle the cold "Inside" the colony, they cannot handle it outside.

Successful beekeeping is a combination of a lot of things and activities: from feeding to good hives, seasons, and pest control. Hence, the reason all beekeepers have to become mindful of particular information on how to keep bees safe. You don't have to learn all these details at once or in one day; that's not the best way to learn. But, you will need to gain knowledge and experience to keep them safe. This book is designed so that you can steadily work through it, one section at a time. That way, you'll gradually feel more confident. The success you will get from this book hinges on your understanding of one concept and then another.

Now that I have talked about seasons, take some time to digest the information (with the others after reading each chapter) then act on what you learned. By doing this, by taking such strategic steps, you will internalize the content of this book and make tremendous progress as a beekeeper. You have done everything right thus far, so what happens next? The harvest!

*You will observe that I repeatedly mentioned "Record book" as a tool you will need for the entire year. Well, the reason for this is that you have to start taking the record from your first beekeeping season.

The data you gather from the first season will help you know what to expect in the next season. Although all seasons are not the same, some things never change, and bees are pretty predictable from one season to the next.

Chapter Six:
All About the Harvest

The word "Harvest" is like music to a beekeeper's ears because it represents a time when all the hard work comes to fruition. Harvest season is a time when the results of the beekeeping process are gained, and the beekeeper can get bee products. However, the only beekeepers who will enjoy the harvest stage are those who have put in the work: if you follow through with all the ideas in previous chapters, then you are ready for the harvest.

The process of harvesting honey is the most enjoyable task for a beekeeper, and after your first harvest, the process becomes simplified from that moment. There are some caveats every beekeeper should know when it comes to harvesting honey (especially as a beginner beekeeper).

You need to know the right time for the harvest, the tools to use, how to filter the brood, and how to keep the hive safe while harvesting. Knowing what to do with the honey afterward is also crucial. The objective of this chapter is to empower you with information that will help you get the best out of the process so that, when it is time to harvest your honey, you will feel confident doing it the right way.

Before harvesting, you must examine the brood to ensure that there is honey on the outer frames. If there isn't any, you may have to let go of some honey for the well-being of the bees: it would be tragic if you enjoy a harvest while your bees starve in winter.

More so, you should know what blooms in your area in the fall season and anything that affects the proceeds of the season in that year. The best food you can give the bees in your hive is their honey; hence the reason that, before harvesting, you must ascertain if they have enough food. A significant reason you should feed your bees with honey from your hive is that when you get honey from another colony, there is a potential for contamination.

You can wipe out your entire colony by feeding them contaminated honey. So, even before we get to the harvest steps, you should know that your priority during the harvest is to keep the bees safe (this is more important than the yield itself). The honey is a bonus!

How to Know When It Is Time to Harvest Honey?

Honeybees work hard for their honey: they wouldn't want to give you any hints that the product is ready to be harvested, so how can a beekeeper know when it is available for harvest? The answer lies in observation! During nectar flow, you have to interrupt them to monitor their progress (do this every two to three weeks). Check the supers to see if the bees have filled the comb with nectar.

When the nectar is at 80% moisture level, you can call the product "Honey." At this stage, the bees will cap it, so check to see if the honey has been capped, and while you can still harvest uncapped honey, it shouldn't be runny. To determine if it is capped or not, turn the frame on its side and shake it: if you see some droplets after the first shake, then the honey is not ready. If there are no droplets, you can go ahead.

Consider the botanical levels

You can also tell if your honey is ready to be harvested by considering the botanical levels of the area around the hive. Consider the primary source of nectar in your hive area: fruit trees, or other plants? You have to understand how they blossom and how long it takes for them to stay in bloom because the best time to harvest honey is towards the end of the nectar flow season.

The end of the nectar flow season signifies a time when the bees have stocked up, and you will have a surplus of honey. The flowers that bloom during spring provide the honey you will harvest at the end of summer. As such, a good beekeeper has to ensure that there's enough honey for the bees during winter.

The tools you need to harvest honey

- You will need:
- **Protective gear:** This includes beekeeping suits, gloves, a jacket, veil, boots, and other protective clothing that protects you from a bee sting.
- **Smoker:** A smoker is significant during harvest as it is also protective gear. You will use the smoker to break up the pheromone signals, get the bees to fill up on honey, and make the harvest process easier.
- **Hive tool:** Don't go harvesting without your hive tools as bees can bind the openings, the hive tool will help you pry through the frames to reach the honey.

- **Bee escape:** Although this is optional, it can help you keep bees away from the supers, which also reduces your harvest time. However, if you use this tool, you must set it up a day before the harvest.
- **Bee brush:** While harvesting, some of the bees will hang on to the honeycomb, the bee brush will help you keep them off the capped honey. The bee brush also lets you keep the bees safe inside the hive while you harvest. The brushes are soft and won't squash the bees.
- **Empty supers:** you can either use empty supers or a large bucket for extraction. You can place the honeycombs in the bucket or get supers to put the frames when you brush off the bees.

You can get all honey harvesting tools in local bee shops.

Steps on How to Harvest Honey

Step one: Examine the hive

The first step for harvesting is to explore the hive to ensure it is the right time for harvest. Do not harvest the honey until the hives reach 80% cap, which means the bees plug the combs in the hive for storage. When the hive is at 80%, it means the combs have been plugged, but if it is less than 80%, the honey cannot be harvested, and you may end up with lousy honey production in the future. The bees may stop producing honey entirely if you collect below 80% cap, so a visual inspection is essential.

You can utilize a measuring tape to get an accurate estimation: measure the capped space and compare it to the uncapped area if it is a ratio of 4 to 1, you are good to go.

Step two: Consider the calendar

You also have to consider the times and seasons for harvesting because it varies based on your location. While some beekeepers only get to harvest once a year, some others in the Northern hemisphere may harvest three times (July, August, and September). In colder climates, it is reasonable to have beehives that allow bees to live inside deep double frames, ready for harvest when both frames are full of honey and capped for winter. But do not take excess honey because the bees will need food in winter.

Step three: Clean yourself

Before harvesting, please make sure you are not wearing any perfume or scented deodorant. If you do, the scent will attract the bees, pique their curiosity, and make them come closer to you (you don't want this). Do not wear any perfume on that day, so if you are coming from a party or elsewhere, you might want to take a shower before harvesting.

Step four: Use your protective gear

While honeybees are not aggressive creatures, opening their hive and removing their honeycomb may trigger them, so to avoid any unpleasant situations, please wear your protective gear. Wear a full beekeeping suit with a long sleeve shirt and long trousers (denim and flannel are right for this situation). Wear heavy shoes, long gloves that go up to your wrists, and an apiculture hat. Also, make sure you go with the right tools: you don't want to start harvesting and remember you didn't come with a tool (it's time-wasting).

Step five: Open the hive

Open the hives one at a time, and as you do so, work with gradual movements because you must keep the bees safe. Using a smoker, puff the smoke from behind around the entrance of the hive. Remove the top and smoke the opening as well to drive the bees further down into the hive. The smoker will also prevent the bees from releasing a pheromone. You may need a mini crowbar hive tool to pry open the inner cover because the bees tend to seal this part with propolis.

Step six: Remove the frames and supers

After getting the bees out of the way, you can remove the frames and supers of the hives. If you are working with only one hive, then it would be straightforward as you will only get out one or two frames. But if you have multiple hives, set the frames and supers 50 feet away from each other and cover them. You can cover the frames with a blanket to prevent the bees from coming back, and then close the hive.

Step seven: Uncap the honeycombs

Uncap the wax-sealed honeycomb by using an uncapping knife or a scratcher to work on both sides of the frames. You can use any uncapping tool at your disposal as you get the content into an extractor. Uncap the honeycombs based on how they fit into the extractor (don't try to overdo it as you may lose honey).

Step eight: Extract the honey

The honey extractor is also crucial but not compulsory while harvesting honey; you use it after opening the honeycombs. Simply turn on the power, place it over the honeycomb and extract the honey. But you can still get your honey without an extractor, hence the reason it isn't compulsory. Some beekeepers who do not use an extractor, get their honey by placing the combs on a pan and applying pressure.

Step nine: Strain and bottle the honey

The last step entails straining and bottling the honey. Use layers of cheesecloth on the honey to get rid of foreign objects, and after filtration, you can bottle the honey. Let the bottled honey sit for a few days to let the air bubbles settle before use.

Thoroughly wash the bottles and jars you will use before pouring honey into them and then remember to replace the comb. You don't have to clean the frames before returning them as the bees will do that. If your beehive is undergoing treatment, please do not harvest its honey as the antibiotics, chemicals, and other medications may be too toxic for the honey. If you must treat the hive, then do it long before the harvest.

Step ten: Aim for quality over quantity

The amount of honey you get from the harvest isn't as significant as the quality. Focus more on quality than quantity. You can measure the quality of your honey by observing its color, flavor, the bees, and foraging behavior.

Over 300 varieties of honey exist all around the world, with each range influenced by a geographic factor, soil condition, plant life, feeding patterns, and harvest season. The official color for honey set by the National Honey Board includes:

- White
- Amber
- Dark amber
- Light amber
- Extra-light amber
- Water-white

In addition to the color recommendations above, you can also use the honey's flavor to ascertain its quality. Compare notes and make observations about the honey you harvested with other beekeepers, and if you observe anything strange with the taste, don't ignore it; carry out an investigation.

How often should I harvest honey?

The frequency of harvesting honey depends on several factors. For example, you have to consider the length of winter, the variety of blooms the bees enjoy in spring, and the hive's temperature. You also have to consider the extent of exposure or vulnerability of the bees to pests and diseases.

However, when all conditions are right, you can expect a harvest every year (after the first year and, in some cases, you may harvest twice a year). If you have a subsequent harvest, exceptional yields will happen based on the weather conditions and availability of nectar. With climate change on the rise, the frequency of the harvest may be affected.

Here is a tip on how to determine the frequency of your harvest: since you may not harvest in the first year, use that time to monitor all these factors. Get to know how the temperature in your hive affects the bees' production of honey, the quality of the nectar, the weather, and other factors. Record your findings and use the details to monitor your next harvest.

Harvesting and the concept of patience

Lastly, you should know that patience is required during harvest season, as every season may not be the same. This book provides a guide to standard seasons, but unusual conditions can happen, and weather and seasons may change. Everything shared in this book and this chapter, in particular, shows you how it "Should" be, but there could be seasonal alterations. You need to be a patient harvester if things are delayed a bit.

Remember that you shouldn't expect a harvest in the first year (I talked about the first-year blues). Yes, there is a possibility of harvesting honey in the first year, but this is not always the case: use the first year to learn more about the beekeeping process and get ready to harvest from the second year.

In this chapter, I focused on harvesting honey because this is a beginners' guide, and honey is the most common commodity from bees. Yes, other bee-related products can be gained from the hive, such as wax, but as a beginner focusing on such extensive harvesting processes may be overwhelming.

As you get better on your beekeeping journey and as you interact with other beekeepers, you will learn how to harvest other products. There may be no demand for other bee products in some localities, so discover what is obtainable in your area first (unless you want it for personal use).

Please focus on honey as the first by-product of bees, and then when you perfect the honey-harvesting process, you can take steps further by getting other products. After harvesting the honey, you can move on to start another beekeeping season using the ideas in previous chapters.

From Chapter One until this section, I considered the practical aspects of beekeeping. Moving on from the practical sections now, we will consider all you should do post-harvest and how to maintain your beehive. The subsequent chapters after this one look at ideas on pest control, beekeeping tools, cleaning processes, and avoiding mistakes. Let us begin with how to handle parasites, predators, and diseases.

Chapter Seven:
Handling Parasites, Predators, and Diseases

Regardless of how excellent you are as a beekeeper, you cannot wholly avoid nature's cycle of habitation, which entails creatures like bees and pests cohabiting in the same space. There will always be pests, predators, and bees that will be vulnerable to diseases, but this doesn't mean you are helpless: you can protect your hive from such damaging exposure. Here, I will talk about how to keep your bees safe from parasites, how to handle predators who try to attack your hive, and all about beekeeping disease control.

The Most Effective Practices to Eliminate Pests and Disease-Spreading Organisms in Bees

Bee pests are a severe threat to any hive and threaten to destroy the beekeeper's hard work. These pests are the agents of disease transmission into honeybees; thus, all beekeepers must be alert and learn how to curb the pests.

When dealing with pests, predators, and diseases in beehives, the most profound approach to use is "Prevention." As a beekeeper, you shouldn't wait until pests invade your hive before taking action: if you wait, by the time you are ready to take action, it might be too late. Below I will discuss some of the best ways of ensuring the safety of the beehive:

The beekeeping community

The beekeeping community is also a powerful force when dealing with pests and predators. When you join such communities, you will be empowered with information on how you can protect your beehive within that locality. You will have first-hand knowledge from the real-time experiences of fellow beekeepers who succeeded in keeping predators and pests away. Beekeepers all have the same goal, and communities are a platform for shared ideas on how to manage the pest and disease situation in the hives. You can maximize the power of the beekeeping community by:

- Becoming a member of a local beekeepers' club will give you access to resources and ideas on how to manage your hive.
- Report abandoned hives to the beekeeping regulators as these abandoned hives could become breeding grounds for pests.
- Your licenses should be up to date and renew all membership fees before expiration.
- You can also join online beekeeping communities and stay connected to a global group.

Genetic control

Genetic controls help keep the pests and parasites away from the beehive, as research shows that there is a relationship between resistance to certain diseases and genetics. Some bee species resist certain conditions while others are highly vulnerable, some species have a more vigorous defense against pests and diseases.

Now that you know this, when you go bee shopping, always purchase the brood that is resistant to diseases. Consider bees that can resist varroa mites and those that can withstand the influence of specific predators.

Mechanical control

Beekeepers can also use mechanical measures to keep pests and predators away, and these are practical steps:

- You can use drone brood trapping to reduce varroa mite infestation.
- The hive box should be elevated and protected to keep mice and other predators away. When you raise the box, you will also get sufficient air inside it and prevent moisture from building inside the hive.
- Make sure you've got screened bottoms to protect the hive from all sides.
- All holes should be sealed to deter arthropod pests and other small insects from getting into the hive box.

Sanitation

Nothing can replace the importance of sanitation to the health and safety of your beehive. Bees do a great job with hive hygiene, but the beekeeper needs to also become proactive with hygienic and healthy routines in the hive. Some of the sanitation practices you can imbibe includes:

- Sanitizing all beekeeping tools after working on the colony. Use the flame of isopropyl alcohol for cleaning purposes, and if a tool is not properly cleaned, it shouldn't be used until it is well-cleaned.

- You can also use a 10% bleach solution to clean your beekeeping clothes and gloves. Dispose of the clothes and gloves if you cannot sanitize them properly, as this will prevent pathogens and pests from transmitting the disease to the hives.
- If you work on the colony with your bare hands, make sure you wash your hands thoroughly afterward. You can rub your hands with alcohol then rinse with warm water and soap.
- If you suspect that the hive has been compromised, then take the necessary steps to isolate the infected area and treat it.

Cultural control

Cultural control is one of the most productive ways of keeping beehives safe from predators, and it is also a cost-effective process. Cultural control is also a preventive way of keeping your beehive safe (taking action before the problem happens). You can maximize cultural control in varying ways:

- When you buy packaged bees, ask for evidence that shows the colony's health, pathogenic and pest control measures. If you are dealing with an authentic seller, he/she will willingly provide evidence. The bees you buy must have been treated for pests and diseases before buying.
- The honey frames should not be interchanged between hives if you think there are pathogens and parasites in another one. If you must recycle frames, then they should be treated and free form pests.

- When buying bee equipment, make sure professionals certify them, as this guarantees safety for your hive from day one.
- If a hive box is infected, then it should be labeled and treated before reuse. The labeling will help prevent the spread of diseases and pests and make it easier for you to separate the infected box from the safe box.
- All beekeeping equipment not in use should be stored in a neat and clean environment.

Colony health

To ensure the safety of your beehive, you will need to ensure that the bee colony is healthy: the healthier the colony, the stronger the bees will be to fight off predators. So now you are wondering, "How can I ensure a healthy stock of bees?"

Start by taking regular checks and inspections seriously; the brood combs should be inspected to ascertain its health (if you can, please do this daily).

Also, monitor the hive for Varroa mites, as these are some of the most damaging predators. They really can weaken the colony's immunity.

Check the hive for rodent invasion by looking for signs of burrows or chewed food. Also, check for stolen honey frames, damaged frames, or exposed hive lids. Remember how you left the hive the previous day, and when you visit the next day, check if anything's changed.

Check the food reserve of the colony: predators will always go for the food reserve. If they are attacking the food reserve, you will know through observation. You should also feed the hive if that's necessary. Always check the weight of the colony; if it is light, then it means food is reducing.

How To Keep The Beehives Healthy

There are steps to maintain the health of the beehives, which includes:

Requeen the hive regularly as this will prevent the bees from getting weaker and dying. The health and strength of the beehive are crucial in fighting off diseases. If your beehive is weak, the bees will start to die, robber bees will become prevalent, diseases will spread quickly, and pests will invade the hive.

Always source all beekeeping equipment and tools from disease-free apiaries. Do not rely on online presence, ads, or reviews to determine where you buy tools. Find out from other buyers and ask the right questions when considering a place to purchase tools.

Regular inspections are also crucial: always inspect the brood frames and honey for signs of distress, diseases, and pests. You can also submit your honey samples and brood combs to labs for inspection and analysis. If you find a suspicious pest around the hive (maybe one you haven't seen before), submit it for review and ascertain if it is a new invasion into the bee space).

Utilize queen excluders to confine brood cells to the brood box: this will prevent them from mixing with the honey cells.

Do not feed untreated honey products to bees. Some untreated bee feeds may contain fungi or bacteria. The pollen you feed bees must be treated. However, if you are unsure of the health of the feeds, use sugar syrup as this is a safer option.

You can also maintain your hive's health by paying close attention to the records you keep from your inspections and observations. This realization is the reason why I recommended you getting a record book. Through the record you keep, you can spot predators' patterns: when they show up, their method of attack, and the seasons when your bees are most vulnerable.

Additional tips on how to keep the pests and diseases out

You can also keep your beehive safe by deciding on the biosecurity goals you want to attain. Write down your goals and be committed to the process regularly. You can use the ideas I shared to keep your bees safe and remember that consistency is also essential for success with the process.

As you continue on your beekeeping journey, remember to train your staff members (if you have staff later) if you decide to expand your hive. Your staff and those around the colony should be aware of your biosecurity standard to protect the bees.

You've got to know the signs of distress, diseases, and abnormalities in your hive, and the way to get it right is through consistent observation.

To reduce the spread of disease in the colony, please prevent swarming.

The Most Common Bee Predators

Raccoons

Raccoons may not be common around your hive, but they are a common predator in most bee areas. They can inflict considerable damage to a beehive if they invade because they feed on bees and honey. Although smaller in size, the raccoon is similar to the bear, it has the power to knock down the hive, climb over it and invade the frames.

You can tell that a raccoon has gained entry into your hive when you see broken frames and tampered honey. You can keep raccoons away with plywood filled with nails on one side and placed at the front of the hive.

The sharp nails on the plywood will protect the hive when the raccoon shows up and is hurt by the nails. However, if you use this method, ensure that you take out the plywood before inspection, feeding, or harvesting at the hive (you don't want to get hurt while protecting your bees).

Birds

Birds are a threat to bees, especially in Asian and African regions. The bee-eater and wax-eater birds are the most common beehive predators that invade hives. They can overturn the colonies and expose the bees and honey to danger.

After overturning them, the birds then feast on the bees and honey. Most of these predator birds are in the USA in particular, and North America in general, and they include shrikes, titmice, flycatchers, and swifts. The most notorious one is the woodpecker that sits near the hive and eats the bees while digging its way into the hive to get the honey.

The woodpecker consumes the bees, destroys the hive, and ruins the hard work of the keeper. Woodpeckers will most likely attack in winter when they can't find insects, so be extra vigilant during the cold seasons. You can keep bird predators away by building a barrier over the hive or use a motion detector to know when they are around; the motion detector can be linked to a flashlight, which will help keep the birds away. In some cases, beekeepers use a scarecrow to keep birds away from the hive.

Wasps and hornets

Wasps and hornets are common threats to bees, and the most worrisome species is the Genus Vespa. The wasps attack the bee colonies, and they are a significant reason why bees abandon their hives. They always target weaker colonies and destroy the entire hive. Wasps also invade the colonies and cause damage to apiaries by first attacking slow-flying bees.

The wasps and hornets attack one bee at a time, starting at the hive's entrance. This is swiftly followed by an onslaught where more than twenty to thirty wasps invade the colony. The predators attack the worker bees, consume the honey, and abscond with surplus brood.

To prevent the wasps and hornet attacks, you will need to install bait-trapping at the hive's entrance and use protective screens. You can also trail one wasp back to its nest and destroy the entire wasp nest. Although hunting the wasps is time-consuming, it is an effective way of destroying the whole brood to prevent a future attack.

A narrower hive entrance is also helpful against wasps and hornets, as it prevents predators from entering the hive in the first place.

Black bear

Now, you know Winnie the Pooh likes honey! Real bears love honey too, and, in their search for it, they will destroy a hive. In the United States of America, the Northwest, Southwest, and Southeast areas are bear habitats; hence, the reason why hives in those areas are susceptible to bear invasion. To keep black bears away, you will need an electric fence that should be erected before bringing the bees to the hive. The electric fence will keep the bears away and keep the colonies safe.

Ants

Ants are the most common predators of honeybees; they live as social creatures, invade the colonies, and take everything from the hive. They can take the honey, dead bees, living bees, the brood, and the queen. In some cases, ants also attack the beekeepers. Furthermore, when a bee colony is under attack from ants, the bees become aggressive, and this might also make them angry at the keeper. You could find yourself being attacked by both sides! To deal with an ant infestation, you must search out their nests within the hive and destroy them.

Burn the ant nests and raise the hive with posts that have been greased with oil (the ants cannot climb into the hive with oil on the posts). You can also place the colony on plastic containers filled with oil or water, as these keep the ants away.

Amphibians

They might not be the first creature that springs to mind, but amphibians are a severe threat to bees. Toads and frogs forage on bees, and if you are not paying close attention to the bees, you may not spot the damage done by amphibians. These amphibians attack at night when no one monitors the hive, but the damage they cause can be easily detected: check for dark brown droppings around the colony.

The amphibians also scatter around the hive entrance, so when inspecting, check the hive's entrance and monitor inside the hive. If you don't get rid of the amphibians, they will weaken the colonies with persistent attacks until the entire hive is unable to survive.

Humans

Well, the fact that you love bees enough to breed them doesn't mean everyone feels the same way. This realization is why human beings are also on the threat list because, surprisingly, they are the most notorious bee predators.

Human beings can steal and vandalize beehives when they consider the bees as "Pests." Most beekeepers have had their hives demolished, stolen, and even burnt, which leads to a complete loss of bees and all the hard work that went into breeding them.

To avoid such human terrorism, beekeepers should breed bees in areas surrounded by people who love bees. You must inform your neighbors of the hive before setting it up, as this will help them adapt to it without feeling threatened.

Some human beings who react negatively to bees out of fear of being stung, but if you inform and educate your neighbors, they will know and do better. Please do not place beehives close to occupied buildings or along human walkways; these are personal spaces that shouldn't be close to a hive.

For additional protection, erect a foot barricade to keep the bees away, and you can also build barriers. Barriers could be brick walls, shrubs, a flower wall, or any form of solid fencing, also place bees where there is a small roof over them, so they don't fly across properties.

Keep your bee's source of water close by so they don't look for water elsewhere. A lack of access to water nearby will make the bees venture further afield, and this may take them to your neighbors' swimming pools or water sources. Also, change the water daily to prevent mosquitoes from breeding in there and avoiding stagnation.

Maintain proper bee management to avoid swarming; most importantly, sharing is caring. Sharing some honey with neighbors after harvesting is a good way to make them bee-tolerant.

Bees are vulnerable to attacks from numerous pests and predators. Although they have developed a natural defense mechanism to protect themselves, it is still the beekeeper's responsibility to keep them safe. The safety measures you take will complement the steps taken by the bees to defend themselves, and you have to be alert to these threats every day.

Just as you learn how to harvest honey, create hives, and even the economic viability of bee products, you have to know how to keep the bees safe. If predators consistently attack your beehive and you do nothing, our honey will be contaminated even if you still have your hive. Your colonies will be weak if you don't protect your bees, and weak colonies will only produce harmful honey.

A more substantial bee colony will defend itself from predators, produce honey at optimal levels, and live longer. This chapter has introduced the predators and pests you should be mindful of as well as how to keep your hive safe. As you continue on your beekeeping journey, you will learn more about the best ways to keep your hive safe in your particular breeding environment.

What are the essential beekeeping supplies for a beekeeper? Is it possible to substitute specific tools or avoid using them entirely? Can beginner beekeepers start with some tools and get more as they continue? Let's find answers in the next chapter.

*If you paid close attention to this chapter, you will find that I didn't talk about using pesticides for pest control. That's because they are harmful to bees. Most pesticides contain chemicals that affect the bees negatively and are poisonous to the honey. Please be mindful of pesticides!

Chapter Eight:
Essential Beekeeping Supplies for Beginners

Talking about the maintenance issue, you've got to know the supplies and tools needed to keep your hive safe. However, there is a lot of information on this topic, and sometimes these excessive ideas can be overwhelming. Here, we will consider the most essential (keyword here is vital) supplies, materials, and tools you should use in your beehive.

Now, I mentioned some of these items passively in previous chapters because I talked about activities like harvesting and inspection where these tools are needed. But, in this chapter, I will highlight these supplies more comprehensively by focusing on how they help you get the best out of the hive and how you can use them.

Please note that it is not an exhaustive list because some beekeepers also use DIY tools for their hives, while others use different tools in their locality when they cannot find some specific tools. The list below covers the essential materials and the ones you can quickly get from wherever your hive is located.

Are you ready to start shopping for bee supplies? Let's go!

Bee Jacket or Suit

No beekeeper wants to get stung, and this is why a bee jacket or suit is essential. From the start of your beekeeping process, you must wear your protective gear to stay safe from the stings. A full suit is recommended, as this will cover most of your body parts, and if you can only get a jacket, make sure the other parts of your body are covered.

Now, in some cases, the beekeeper's suit may be too expensive for a beginner, which means you need to think about other full-body protective options. If you've got a thick cameo jacket, good jeans, or an overall, you can use these to stay safe.

If you join the beekeepers' association before you start the beekeeping process itself, you might get some protective suits from more experienced keepers with several outfits they no longer use.

This protective gear is the first on the list because it is vital, you should only get other supplies after getting this one. Also, look out for suits with pockets as these will help you keep your tools close by during inspections.

Rubber Boots

Many beekeepers have hurtful stories about how bees attack their legs because they wore regular shoes on their beekeeping ventures. You can avoid such negative experiences by getting the right boots. More so, all beekeepers can prevent the bees from crawling their pant legs. Rubber boots are also an excellent option for cold weather inspections or when you have to take care of the bees in the rain.

You cannot dig through a beehive successfully without covering your legs completely, and if you cannot get rubber boots, get protective boots. You can also get shoes made of hard material, shoes that are impregnable and sustainable. Look out for shoes with a solid sole so you can use them for a long time.

One of the good things about such beekeeping tools is the fact that you can use them for other activities aside from beekeeping. If you do get rubber boots and maintain them, you can use them for years without needing to buy new ones.

Gloves

Gloves are inexpensive beekeeping tools that keep you safe while working in the hive. Some beekeeping suits come with gloves, and others do not: regardless of this option, buy a good pair of gloves. With beekeeping gloves, you will want to buy a sturdy material, one that is not easily prone to getting torn on the job.

While some beekeepers prefer goatskin gloves, others prefer rubber gloves, and there are several other options available in beekeeping stores. Leather gloves are also preferred because they allow for proper ventilation above the wrist. Regardless of the product, make sure you get suitable gloves to protect you as you interact with the bees.

Hive tool

Next is the hive tool, which is essential because it is a multi-purpose beekeeping tool. The hive tool is a simple flat metal bar crafted to make openings or to scrape things. You can use this tool to open hives, inspect frames, and scrape stuff off the bee box.

Bees use propolis to glue things together inside the hive; as such, it makes it challenging for beekeepers to check the colony when they want to inspect it or during harvest. Most hive tools are painted in bright colors for visibility, and this also makes it harder to misplace them.

With the hive tool, you can unseal those areas, separate the combs from the sides of the hive, cut and scrape off the propolis. A hive tool that comes with a knife on one side and the primary hive tool on another side is a popular choice with beekeepers. More so, the hive tool is suitable for all kinds of beehive designs.

There are various types of hive tools, when you go shopping for hive tools, you will find different types, and they all do the same job. To avoid getting confused, you can ask the seller to recommend one for you. Hive tools are also one of the most inexpensive beekeeping tools and can be used for a long time.

Smoker

A smoker is on the priority list for essential bee tools as they are used to mask pheromones released by bees, and they are great for moving the bees away while you inspect or harvest. The smoke from the smoker also calms the bees, thus making your beekeeping process easier.

The psychology behind using the smoker is that it makes the bees believe there is a fire, which makes them gorge on honey, preparing for relocation. When the bees are full, they tend to move slowly and will most likely not sting because they can't move the tip of their abdomen.

Additionally, the smoker is made of stainless steel and has a heat shield with a grate at its lower sides. You have various smoker options: you can use wood pellets, corn cobs, pine needles, burlaps, or dried grass. When buying a smoker, do NOT use one that has been chemically treated as this can affect the bees negatively.

The fact that the smoker is made of metal means it can become scorching when it is in use; as such, you MUST be careful when handling it. Also, avoid overloading the smoker, especially during lighting, as this can hurt your hands or protective gear.

Although the smoke doesn't normally hurt the bees, it can become harmful when used excessively in the hive. This is why, when I talked about harvesting, I only said use the smoker for a few seconds. This tool aims to get the bees out of the way and not to kill them.

Lastly, choose a smoker you can afford (there are several types of smokers out there), but effectiveness is not influenced by price.

Bee brush

A bee brush is made up of soft bristles used to get bees out of the frame without harming them. This brush is used when moving the frames from one hive to another, and when harvesting honey. While it is possible to shake some of the bees off the frame, some others might still hold on to the frame, and this is when you will need the brush. If you don't have access to a proper bee brush, then you can use an unused paintbrush (but since it will probably cost just as much as the bee brush, you should try and get one).

Informative Books

When it comes to successful beekeeping, education is the key, as even experienced beekeepers still read books to learn more about current beekeeping trends. You have started this journey the right way with this book, but reading doesn't stop when you get started.

You've got to continually read books about beekeeping to stay updated on what's happening in the sector. For example, if you start beekeeping today, some of the steps you are taking now may be modified in the future. If you don't adjust your beekeeping approaches to suit the modernized trend, you will be left behind.

Books also provide ideas on how you can achieve better results with your hive because beekeeping is always changing. Lots of research through books will help you know the next steps to take and how to get things right from season to season.

Some beekeepers cannot make productive decisions because they don't read, so they don't know what to do when faced with a pest, predator, or disease challenge. But, a beekeeper who reads and understands how the beekeeping world works, will take action at the right time because of the wealth of knowledge he or she has gained through books.

Beekeeper's veil

A beekeeper's veil is also essential as it protects you from getting stung on your face. This item can either be bought separately or together with a beekeeper's suit.

Uncapping tool

This tool is optional, but it helps when you want to keep the honeycomb on the frame without the bees drawing out a new comb. This tool enables you to get the caps off the comb: it is sometimes called an uncapping fork or uncapping knife and is efficient during a harvest.

Honey extractor

The honey extractor is a "Must-have" tool, and since you may not be harvesting honey in your first year as a beekeeper, you can save towards buying it the second year. With a honey extractor, you can collect honey from the honeycombs without hurting them, and there are various kinds of honey extractors on the market.

You can buy stainless steel or a plastic extractor: plastic extractors are not as popular as the meal ones because they don't last long. The stainless-steel extractor is food-safe, more reliable, and durable. The extractor's capacity also varies, with some having two frames, three frames, and even up to ten frames.

The capacity you go for should be based on the size of your bee production: if you are going to pivot from one beehive to five, you will need a bigger honey extractor. Most beginners go with the two-frame honey extractor because it is affordable.

The honey extractor comes with two mechanisms: radial and tangential. The tangential extractor spins the combs one side at a time as the frame is removed, and the radial turns the frames, thus completing the process. Although there are other manual ways of extracting the honey from the honeycomb, if you can afford an extractor, please get one.

Bee feeders

Bee feeders are tools you use to feed the bees, especially when nectar is insufficient (mostly during winter months). While there are different types of bee feeders, it is crucial to get one that suits your peculiar hive environment. You can use the division board feeder, which lies close to the clustering bees or use the entrance feeders placed close to the hive's entrance.

Queen catcher

Queen catchers are handy tools that help separate the queen for a while, especially when you are inspecting the hive or cleaning. If you don't want to lose the queen, you will have to keep her in a catcher until you can place her back into the hive.

This tool is also crucial if you want to catch a swarm of bees because the bees will go wherever the queen goes, so all you have to do is get the queen in the catcher, and the bees will follow.

How to choose the right tools?

Always go for tools that will last a long time because this will help you save money long-term. If you work closely with the local beekeeper's association, you will know the right stores and online platforms to make your purchases. Genuine sellers will give you a warranty for bigger and more expensive items.

Sometimes, with beehive tools and supplies, prices may be misleading, so please pay attention to the quality of functionality. Prices will always vary, so don't use cost as the yardstick all the time: go for quality, and check the product reviews, before making a purchase.

To succeed at beekeeping, you've got to become conversant with everything you will need even before getting started. Of course, as your hive grows bigger, and if you decide to expand it, you will need additional tools, but for now, those are the materials you will need.

We cannot complete our beekeeping journey without talking about the cleaning processes for a typical beehive. You will gain answers to questions like when to clean, how to clean, and the products to use in the next chapter.

Chapter Nine:
Beekeeping Cleaning Procedures

Whatever you take seriously has to be maintained appropriately, hence the reason you must pay close attention to cleaning. This chapter concentrates on all aspects of the beekeeping cleaning process and pays close attention to the essential elements of cleaning a beehive.

The honeybee colonies are vulnerable to infection and infestation from a wide range of pests and diseases. These infestations happen because of bacteria, fungi, viruses, and insects such as mites. Honeybees are also at risk of epidemics; it is crucial to know the signs of these pests and take care of the hive using effective cleaning procedures.

Good hygiene is a crucial step in reducing the spread of infection, but, before I get started, there are some things you should note. First, you must clean and sterilize your hives and equipment because these are materials that come in contact with bees and the honey.

Next, you must have all the cleaning tools before you start cleaning, and this includes eye protection, waterproof gloves, steel-capped boots, and other materials. If you will need help before cleaning day, get someone to help you (you can get help from your local beekeeping association). If you MUST use chemically infused cleaning tools, please take all precautions advised by the manufacturers (they also know that bees are vulnerable to chemicals).

So, when should you clean and sterilize your beekeeping equipment?

- Clean your equipment when you bring it out from storage or the field.
- Sterilize your cleaning kits when the colonies experience an infection or infestation.
- Before you use or reuse spare or empty hives, sterilize them.
- If you use any item exposed to disease, please clean it before reusing it.
- Whenever you move things between colonies, wash them. Note, even healthy colonies can harbor destructive organisms that cause diseases. For example, the bacteria responsible for EFB, and spore bacterium that causes AFB can exist in combs for an extended period without being detected. Hence, the reason you must be conscientious about beehive hygiene is because some diseases do not always manifest immediately.
- Always clean hive tools with washing soda after use in the hive.

It may not always be safe to clean, disinfect, and reuse beekeeping equipment after it is contaminated. If the contamination is severe, sometimes you may have to dispose of the tools and get new ones.

In Chapter Two, I mentioned that there are different types of beehives, but the most common are wooden hives. I'm now going to discuss how to disinfect a wooden hive. I will also talk about how to clean other kinds of colonies as we go on.

- How to clean and disinfect wooden hives:
- Dismantle the hive and place its components in a massive domestic chest freezer (this should be at 20 degrees C) for 48 hours before cleaning.
- Putting the parts in the fridge will kill all insects, pests, and moths.
- Place the parts of the hive onto sheets of cardboard or on newspapers (get the debris out).
- Start scraping the boxes using a hive tool.
- Remove all wax comb and propolis lumps while scraping the box.
- Be careful when cleaning the internal parts and the frames because these are spots that can harbor pests and pathogens.
- If you spot excessive dirt and infestations, then you may want to consider replacing all the frames with new ones entirely.
- If you seek to sterilize the equipment, please remember to remove all plastic runners.
- While scraping, you will find that bits of wax and propolis will fall in the newspaper sheets (destroy all of these discharges). Then clean the scrapper and sterilize it for future use.

I talked about repeatedly sterilizing the hive and wondering how you can make that happen. Well, you can do it in different ways:

Scorching with blowlamp

You can sterilize the brood box using a blowlamp, and when doing this, use the tip of the blue flame to get rid of all propolis on the hive. You can tell the box is appropriately sterilized when the timber darkens to a uniform brown color.

Soda crystals

Soda crystal solution cleans beekeeping equipment: it is also called sodium carbonate. This solution consists of 1 kg washing soda and 5 liters of water with a dash of washing liquid. Immerse the equipment in the mix, use a wire brush to scrub off residues until the tool is clean.

You can also carry out frame sterilization in the same way; get some newspapers on a work surface and scrape the frames in the paper after dipping it in the mixture. Prepare another mixture of soda solution (1:5) in a pan (the pan should be large enough to hold the honey frames).

Boil the water and fill a separate pan with cold water. Submerse the frames in the soda mix for a minute and then put them in the cold water, bring them out, and leave to dry. Reuse the frames after they dry up.

Chemical sterilization with disinfectants

You can sterilize brood boxes, supers, and other beekeeping tools using disinfectants that contain hypochlorite. Sodium hypochlorite is in about 3% of household bleach and immersing this beekeeping equipment in the solution for twenty minutes can kill bacteria.

The solution for immersion should be one-part bleach and five-parts water: the spores should come in contact with the solution. Dip the tools into the mix, bring them out, and allow them to dry. Also, wear protective clothing when using this method.

Acetic acid

You will have to sterilize the comb using evaporation fumes from acetic acid to destroy the wax moth and spores of chalkbrood. You can use this treatment by stacking all beehives and components with combs on a work surface and block off the hive entrance because acetic acid can attack metal.

Put a non-metallic dish on top of the frames. With caution, put 80% acetic acid into the bowl and place an empty hive box on top of the stack. Seal up the empty box at the top of the pile with a hive cover, and seal the joints between the boxes and adhesive tape, so fumes do not escape. Leave the stack that way for about one week to make sure the fumigation is thorough.

After a week, you can remove the acid dishes and air the boxes for at least two days before reusing them. Remember to wear suitable protective clothing while undergoing this cleaning task.

Paraffin wax (By immersion)

This method entails the immersion into hot paraffin wax. The wax should be heated to 160 degrees C for ten minutes, and it shouldn't get to 199 degrees C. If you are unsure about undertaking this method yourself, then get a specialist or seek advice from other beekeepers in your community.

Irradiation

You can sterilize the wooden hive components such as the stored supers and empty combs, using gamma rays from a radioisotope of cobalt. This method kills infective organisms without causing any damage to the hive components. You can reach out to firms that specialize in irradiation to kill foulbrood spores. If you are going to use this approach, please follow the guidelines and recommendations of your local bee inspector.

How to Clean and Disinfect Plastic or Polystyrene Hives

I have talked about how to clean wooden hives, and now I will talk about plastic hives, which have been in use for a long time. Before sterilizing the hive and its components, clean them thoroughly, and, as you did with the wooden hive, freeze the plastic parts.

Remember that the freezing process kills insect pests. Place the components on top of a newspaper on a work surface after freezing. Start scraping all parts of the hive to remove the wax comb, propolis, and other debris.

After cleaning the hive, you can sterilize it, but unlike wooden hives, the sterilizing options for plastic are limited. You cannot use a blowtorch because it will melt the plastic, and you cannot use paraffin wax as well because the temperature will also be too much. This delicate situation with plastic hive means you can only use specific chemical disinfectants that contain caustic soda or hypochlorite.

How To Clean The Queen Excluders

Some beekeepers forget to clean the queen excluder because they focus so much on the other parts of the hive, but this isn't right. The queen excluder needs to be cleaned and sterilized, and there are different ways of doing this, depending on the type of excluder you use.

You can start by removing all debris, just scrape them out with a scraping tool. Also, remove propolis, and, with a wire brush, get rid of wax from the excluder. If you have a wire excluder, then you should scorch it using a blowlamp, but do it carefully, so you don't melt the metal joints.

You can also scrub the excluder with a washing soda solution, which consists of 1 kilogram of soda and 5 liters of water with a dash of washing liquid. Disinfect Plastic excluders in the same way you clean plastic hives. Wear protective clothing when doing this; protect your eyes, and use rubber gloves.

How to Clean Other Minor Equipment

You can use a blowlamp to scorch hive tools, but do not heat them to the extent that you damage them. All plastic equipment or components should be scrubbed clean with a washing soda solution. Some open-ended plastic sheets are tough to clean from the inside so you can seal the open ends before use.

How to Clean Beekeeping Clothing

If you have leather gloves, they may be challenging to clean (this is why beekeepers are not advised to use leather gloves). If you must use them, then wash them with soapy water and then use disposable or rubber gloves going forward.

If you used Wellington boots, then scrub them with a washing soda solution. All other footwear should be cleaned in the same way. Wash off mud, honey splashes, propolis, and all other discharge from beekeeping clothing immediately after using them.

Beekeeping overalls should be regularly washed as you would do with your regular clothes. Mix a small quantity of washing soda crystals and detergent to propolis and make sure all zips are done up to avoid getting damaged while washing.

How to Deal with EFB and AFB

Honeybee hives can be infected by two forms of a bacterial disease known as EFB and AFB. EFB means European Foulbrood, and AFB means American Foulbrood. The sickness is called Foulbrood because these are diseases that affect the brood, consisting of the bee larvae and pupae. These diseases can cause a lot of disruption in the hive.

If you suspect that your hive has these diseases, you have to report it to the National Bee Unit as they can provide a confirmatory diagnosis to ascertain if your colony is in danger. But before the diagnosis is complete, you may have to close the hive and reduce the number of entrances to just one bee space. Next, you must disinfect your beekeeping gloves and all equipment using a reliable solution (washing soda) and move on to examine other colonies.

If the bee unit confirms the presence of AFB, the infected colonies should be burnt before they spread to other areas, and the hive must be sterilized before reuse. While Virkon S is a disinfectant that's effective against non-spore microbes, such as EFB bacteria and viruses, it's not recommended for AFB (only use a hypochlorite-based cleaner such as bleach).

The Destruction of Old and Infected Beehive Tools

Lastly, after cleaning the hives, you may need to burn the infected tools. However, you are not supposed to burn them on the surface of open ground. Dig a pit of about 45 cm and burn them there.

Plastics may not be reusable, especially if they are already damaged. Plastic that has been contaminated can be recycled for future use. You can get the advice of your local bee authority to learn more about recycling beehive tools guidelines. Uninfected materials can also be disposed of at landfill sites but note that this does not apply to infected tools.

If there are other disposable guidelines for bee tools in your locality, please adhere to them. Most of the time, pests remain in a particular area because they inhabit such disposed devices. There are also specialist companies that deal with the disposal of such materials, find out if such companies exist in your locality. Please do not wait until your plastic materials wear entirely out before deciding what to do with them.

How to clean the beehive surroundings

The surrounding environment of the beehive is also important because when the surroundings are dirty, it can attract a lot of pests. Bacteria, fungi, and other diseases also thrive in the filthy environment: sadly, too many beekeepers focus only on the beehive itself. If you have a clean beehive or place a clean bee box in a dirty environment, the dirt outside will find its way into the hive. So how can you keep the environment clean?

Nurture your garden plants

Remember that flowers need bees and bees need flowers; that's the reason you must nurture the right plants around your hive. Please make sure the plants are well-treated; water them and make sure they're looked after.

You may have to feed less of your home-made syrup to the bees if they eat well enough through flower pollination. But, if the environment around the plants is dirty, then it means the plants are unhealthy, and the bees will be feeding on unhealthy nectar.

Keep the surroundings clean, so you can adequately nurture your garden plants for the bees. Get rid of all weeds around the hive and become intentional about planting more flowers for the bees.

Have clean drainage systems

Drainage systems such as gutters around the hive shouldn't be clogged or full of dirt because they can spread bacteria, and the bad odor can spread. The bees need to go out to pollinate flowers, and when they leave their hives, they should be able to feel the fresh air and warmth of nature.

They shouldn't be allowed to feel weak because of bad odors and mosquitoes that breed in dirty gutters and drainage systems. Take responsibility for your hive's environment by becoming proactive with cleaning all areas, including drainage systems.

Clean water sources

It is not enough to clean the water feeder you use in feeding the bees or changing their water; you also need to ensure that the water sources around the hive are clean. If the water sources are dirty, it will ultimately become a breeding ground for mosquitoes (just like the drainage systems). Even if you don't use the water systems around the hive, maybe it is solely meant for the bees, go ahead and clean it! Avoid leakages that could cause mini-floods, which will become a breeding ground for germs.

Remove dead plants and leaves from hive surroundings.

The dead leaves from trees and plants constitute debris around the beehive, and in many cases, they are the hiding places for pests and predators. If there are trees and plants around your hive, then it is understandable that there will be dead leaves.

Please don't wait until such dead leaves pile up before getting rid of them. If you cannot do it daily, then do it weekly (Saturdays can be a good day for general sanitation). Getting rid of debris will also give you a better view of your hive's surroundings so that you know when a predator has attacked.

Well done! You have moved from learning the basic ideas of beekeeping to knowing how to harvest and now to clean. So, you have made tremendous progress thus far, and it is a testament to your commitment to the beekeeping process.

You can always use the details shared in this chapter from the beginner to the experienced beekeeping stage: when you get to the expert stage, you will only have to increase your cleaning supplies. Well, do we end it all here? Of course, not, there is one more section you must read through, which entails a detailed presentation of beekeeping mistakes you must avoid.

Chapter Ten:
Beekeeping Mistakes to Avoid

In this last chapter, I will highlight some of the most common mistakes beginners make that you must avoid. Some of these mistakes are steps some beginners take that lead to severe challenges for their beekeeping venture. This chapter's objective is to help you prevent errors from the start.

Please note some of these mistakes are practices some beekeepers believe to be right but are actually harmful to the beekeeping process. It's better if you can avoid these mistakes and strengthen your hive's long-term health.

Some Beekeeping Mistakes to Avoid

Inspecting the hive too frequently

As a beginner, it is natural to become excited at the prospect of starting a beehive. You have watched a dozen YouTube videos and documentaries waiting for the bees to arrive. So here they are, and you feel the urge to look at them every day. You examine them on the first day and then do the same thing the following day.

You always want to make sure the bees are still there and that they are okay: well, it is thoughtful of you to take care of them. But you should also remember that these are bees who just settled into a new hive, and, as such, they are going through a confusing time.

They are trying to understand their new hive, accept the queen, and excessive inspection involving this strange giant poking into their new home all the time will stress them out. The bees need to feel secure, and ripping the roof over their heads 3-4 times in a week will not help them with that sense of security.

Give the bees time to settle into the hive: you can check on them once a week to make sure they have enough food and then leave them alone for at least two weeks. Imagine if you just moved into a new home, and your landlord shows up every five minutes, asking if you are settling in well enough?

In a new home, you just want to unpack and relax. Even though your landlord has good intentions, you will feel overwhelmed by the consistent visitation. Now imagine this scenario with your bees as the tenant, not sweet, right? Then don't do it!

Using bee traffic as the sole model for assessment

When assessing your beehive, you've got to also consider the hive from outside. Watch how the bees fly out and bring pollen, drink water, and the duration of their pollination. Become familiar with the bees' routine and the traffic to the hive. Pay attention to the number of bees that fly in and out of the colony. When you carry out such an assessment, you will easily spot changes and know when there is a problem.

Despite these assessment levels based on traffic, you also need to monitor the combs by opening the hive and examining the content inside. If you notice a problem on the outside, it has progressed too far on the inside, hence the reason why traffic shouldn't be the sole factor for assessment.

Traffic will only reveal issues with bee movement for you, which means you may not get a full representation of the problems in the beehive, which means there might be other issues. Yes, traffic assessment is excellent, but I am urging you to take the monitoring process even more seriously by considering both traffic and internal evaluation.

Improper inspections

When a beekeeper does a poor job with inspections, it can affect the beehive because the beekeeper has missed out on significant details. When you go for your beehive inspection, what do you do? What do you look out for, and what do you analyze? Do you only look at the hive itself or consider the health of the bees?

Beehive inspection is time to check *everything* about the hive thoroughly from the entrance to the top of the colony and even the surrounding. When you rush the assessment, it means it is done hurriedly and without care. An inspection is not about looking at the hive alone; it is about being intentional with your search.

You have to consider the state of the hive and juxtapose your findings with how it should be. For example, from the information gathered in this book and other materials you use, you should know how the hive is in specific seasons. If you carry out an inspection and the colony looks different from the general expectation, then it is a sign that things are not okay.

Don't rush an assessment! Take your time and get it right with your beehive.

Ignoring a queenless hive

Beehives cannot survive without a queen: although this is a well-known fact, some beekeepers still do not pay attention to the queen's health. Some beekeepers say they have heard stories about colonies that survived without a queen, so they don't take seriously the threat of a hive going down without a queen.

Well, a hive without a queen may survive for a little while; if you look at such hives, from the entrance, you will still see a lot of bees, but move beyond the door. If you take a closer look at the colony and the bees inside, you will start to notice a lot of them are dead.

The weight of the hive will gradually lessen, and soon the colony will be completely demolished. When the queen dies, the weaker bees will start to die before the stronger ones; hence the reason you may still think the lack of a queen doesn't matter.

Another sign of a queenless hive is the lack of eggs and young larvae because the queen lays the eggs that become the larvae. Also, you will notice that your colony has no brood over time, which is a massive problem for any beekeeper. So, what should you look out for to ascertain the health of the queen?

Eggs! You need to look out for eggs in your beehive as this is the proof that the queen bee is alive, healthy, and safe. Finding the eggs means the queen is active and still laying, which is her most important task. Whenever you go for your random hive inspection, look for eggs, and if you check multiple times within two weeks without seeing eggs, that is a sign of trouble.

When you don't respect the bees' space

Bees are very meticulous creatures: they don't like to waste space, and bee space is the gap area in the beehive that the bees won't fill with wax or propolis. If that space is too tiny for them, they will seal it up with propolis, and if it is too broad, they will use it for food storage.

This means that if the bees' space is not well-managed and utilized, they will fill up those spaces with wax and propolis. This idea may not be a big deal to you, but when it is time to inspect the hive, it will be difficult: you will have to use the hive tool to get rid of wax so you can view the brood.

Bees can also be exceedingly messy during nectar flow because they are having a good time with the flowers, eating a lot, and producing a lot. If you don't respect their space by maximizing every area, you will deal with propolis and wax issues.

Failure to feed package bees

Some beekeepers feed their bees sugar too soon, which may affect the bees, but there are some exceptions to these rules, especially when you have to help your bees feed. One such exception is when you buy package bees in spring because when you first get them, they are confused, weak, and without honey.

Sadly, some beginner beekeepers do not feed their new colonies, which makes the bees vulnerable to a lot of health issues. When you get a new territory, you must feed them for at least one month before they get on their feet and start making honey.

If you fail to feed them, you will lose the entire colony by fall season unless your hive is in a nectar-rich area. You have to feed nucleus colonies as well because, just like package bees, they need the complementary feeding process from you before they can start making honey.

But, while feeding them, also inspect the hive to ascertain when they start making their honey. If you notice that after a week of consistent feeding, the bees still haven't started making honey, don't stop feeding them. Overfeeding can lead to swarms, though, so this is something you need to balance carefully.

Leaving out frames

Bees will always build honeycombs in any space, which is why the beehive structure is designed so that the bees get to develop only in the places you want the honey. With a Langstroth hive, for example, it is constructed in two styles to hold eight to ten frames, but if you put fewer frames inside this hive, the bees will build honeycomb on empty spaces.

If you add a super without putting in the frames, you will end up with a box of combs at the roof of the hive (which is a huge mess). If the hive you use stipulates or is structured to hold a certain number of frames, please do not leave out any of the frames.

Make sure all frames are utilized because that is the only way you can have the bees produce honey in the most organized, safe, and healthy manner. Using the frames also makes the bee harvest easier for you as, instead of trying to get honey from all over the hive, you only have to deal with frames and supers.

Not wearing protective gear because you think you are used to the bees.

Even the most docile bees can sting you, and the fact that they are in a new habitat with you as a beginner can make them restless. As such, even if your bee suit is uncomfortable, remember that you need it to stay safe: don't think you have become used to the process and so you can carry out inspections without the suit.

Some beekeepers like to show up at the hive without wearing their suit, and this puts them at risk from the bees. Don't let yourself fall for this kind of pointless bravado. Beekeepers with years of experience are sensible enough to suit up all the time; as a beginner, you need to make this a part of your beekeeping routine.

Remind yourself of the importance of a beekeeping suit by putting it on WHENEVER you go to your hive. Don't compromise on wearing the suit all the time.

Failure to use a smoker

The smoker is an essential beekeeping tool used to distract the bees, and, as crucial as it is, some beekeepers try to skip the process and take on the hive without a smoker. Well, doing that is a mistake because, without the smoker, the bees will react defensively by stinging your suit.

You may also end up killing many of them. It could endanger the people around because anything can happen when the bees are agitated. Think of the smoker as a negotiator that mediates between you and the bees: when you use the smoker, they go about gorging on honey, which gives you time to go about your business without anyone being hurt.

Accidents to Avoid

There are some beekeeping accidents you must avoid, even though you can learn from the process when some of them happen. These are accidents that occur suddenly without you even knowing it sometimes. For example, abruptly dropping the hive while moving it can make the bees agitated. If you lift two beehives at the same time and trip over a bear fence without wearing a bee suit, you will have trouble with the bees.

Some beekeepers can accidentally kill the queen of the colony through starvation because they assumed that the bees were well fed. If you lock up the hive mid-summer and forget to unlock it, you can kill all the bees. Or keepers might end up killing brood larvae mistakenly thinking it is hive beetle larvae.

Don't leave your back door open (If your beehive is in the backyard) during spring because bees can fly into your home. Don't bring the bee comb into your home directly from the hive without cleaning it first (you will bring bees into your house). Know how to differentiate between wasps for bees. Avoid taking your mobile phone with you when you go for bee inspections; the ringtone can irritate them.

There are so many beekeeping accidents that can affect your beehive, and while some accidents are inevitable, you can reduce the frequency of their occurrence. Again, by being careful and cautious of the fact that you are dealing with small, fragile creatures, you can limit the possibilities of such accidents happening.

Starting with only one hive

Do you love cookies? Muffins or some other cake? If you do, you will agree that having one is not enough, and it is the same with beehives! Having more than one hive will help you maintain your beekeeping standards should one colony fail. Think about how you will have to start all over again just because one hive became problematic.

If you start with two hives, you wouldn't have to start all over again; you will move on with the second hive and strengthen it. If one colony appears weak, you can take some brood from the other thriving one to help the struggling colony.

You will be giving your beekeeping project a better chance at survival if you have two hives, as this will also assure you of longevity. You will learn how the beekeeping process works with two different colonies and gain a wealth of experience.

Underestimating the impact of Varroa

"Varroa destructor" is a mite that attacks bees and produces the disease varroosis. Ignoring Varroa doesn't mean it will go away as it is one of the most challenging problems in a beehive. Many experienced beekeepers had to restart a hive multiple times because they underestimated the impact of Varroa on the hive. You can lose dozens and dozens of bee colonies from the devastating effect of varroa mites. It's regarded as a significant factor in reducing the bee population worldwide.

As such, from the beginning, you have to be conscious of these mites by paying close attention to your hive. Do not dismiss signs and symptoms because you want to believe it is not valid: if the bees are showing signs of a problem, take the problem seriously!

There are many varroa control options in the beekeeping market today, so you don't have to worry about managing the situation. But you must combine the varroa treatment with good beekeeping practices and hygiene that keeps the bee safe.

While you may not eliminate the varroa mites, you can reduce their impact by being proactive with varroa control. These mites are known to evolve quickly, and they have gained resistance to control chemicals, which is why beekeepers use a lot of strategies to keep them in check.

Some strategies include breaking up a colony, using small cell foundations to reduce the space available for mites to grow, and being conscious of changes in your hive.

Too much harvest all too soon

The first year the bees spend with you in their new hive is probably the hardest for them because they have to start living in a new environment. They have to accept the queen, learn the terrain of the area, secure a food source, increase their numbers, and store enough food for winter.

Some beekeepers do not take these changes into consideration. They expect too much from the bees and quickly start harvesting the moment they see honey. When the harvest is too soon, the bees will have nothing for winter. While the amount of honey each colony needs varies, new bees will need a lot of honey to survive.

Harvesting too much and too soon when the bees are just getting used to their new environment is a mistake all beekeepers should prevent. Your role in the first few years is to nurture them and keep them safe; if you do your part, the bees will ensure you get a bountiful harvest.

If you don't make the hive a safe place for the bees, if you harvest the honey too soon, they will not survive!

Wrong hive placement

Wrong hive placement is a mistake most beekeepers don't even realize that they do because it has become normalized. Some beekeepers also erroneously think that the beehive's positioning doesn't matter so long it is standing upright, and this is not true.

If your hive is not placed the right way, it can be very uncomfortable for the bees, making them restless and agitated. Placing the beehive whichever way you want will make the hive vulnerable to weather elements such as strong winds and heavy rain.

If the wind is too strong and the colony is not well-placed, it can knock it down, destroying all your hard work.

Ensure that the area allows you to perform your inspection from any angle, cut bushes away, and pests should not be allowed to breed close to the hive. Place the colony farther away from places with foot traffic because you don't want people walking too close to the bees.

When deciding on a site, do not only settle for what suits your needs but also consider the bees. Choose a safe location that is just right for them.

Being okay with limited knowledge on beekeeping

Some beekeepers learned the basic ideas of beekeeping years ago and still rely on the old information while being satisfied with the fact that they have limited knowledge of the subject matter. This lack of interest in learning new information is a huge mistake, and it should be avoided.

If you only have limited beekeeping knowledge, you will not know when trends change, which means you will be living in modern times but stuck in the old ways. The best part about being a beekeeper is learning about bees. They really are fascinating little creatures!

Please do not be content with the information you've received from this book or any other information you've collected. Strive to know more because the beekeeping sector never remains the same: things change all the time, and you should be aware of such changes.

Subscribe to beekeeping newsletters, listen to beekeepers' podcasts, watch beekeeping documentaries, and always be interested in gaining new information about bees.

Spending too much money

Some beginners get so carried away with the excitement of starting a beehive that they buy everything they can find that relates to beekeeping. The problem with this approach is that they end up wasting money on items and tools they wouldn't use: what's the point in having equipment you don't need? Why buy something you don't even know how to use?

Yes, I understand that people can get excited about the prospect of finally getting started with beekeeping. But the pressure to spend money from the beginning will take away the joy of the experience. A lot of beekeepers will lose their hive in the first year because the first year is not always profitable; it is more of a time to learn.

If you spend so much money in that first year and don't even harvest honey, how will you get back the money you spent on the equipment? You can spend more after gaining experience and buying more materials if needed, but as a beginner, you only need the necessary tools.

Rough handling bees

Bees are fragile creatures. Yes, they may seem tough because they sting, but they are sensitive and delicate, and so should be handled carefully. Some beekeepers worry about getting stung by a bee, and this fear drives them into rough handling the bees. When you visit the hive, don't bang things around and knock the bees about carelessly.

This mistake is one of the reasons why some bees become aggressive. When you smash and kill one bee, it releases a pheromone which causes other bees to become aggressive. Always take your time when working with the bees. Be gentle when handling them, as this is crucial to the lifespan of your hive.

Lack of preparedness

Some beekeepers think after they set up the hive, that is all they have to do. They fail to prepare for other beekeeping activities. But a lack of preparedness only leads to mistakes caused by not taking action at the right time.

Don't prepare for harvest season when it is only a day before the harvest, and don't plan for winter when winter starts. A smart beekeeper has to be several steps ahead, and early preparation ensures good results when it comes to beekeeping.

Poor record-keeping

If you don't take notes after inspections and observations, you won't know how to improve your beekeeping practices. Some beekeepers cannot tell when something is wrong with the hive because they don't have a record of previous cases. This mistake causes them to treat every case in isolation and as a new trend: but most challenges with beehives do not happen in isolation.

If you keep proper records, you will realize that during the beekeeping season, your bees are vulnerable to change in the weather or the threat of a disease outbreak. Every time you do a hive inspection, take notes on what you observe, as this will help you learn new things about your hive.

Hive history is crucial for every beekeeper, and it can only be obtained when you take notes regularly. You can tell if you have had more success with one queen breed or another, and the seasons when it seems like the bees produce better honey. You can keep records manually using a notepad or digitally using a "Beekeeper's app," which helps you track all activities in your hive.

Asking the wrong people for help

The quality of advice you get as a beekeeper will affect how you handle your hive. If you are getting information from those who don't know what they are doing, it will result in poor beekeeping. For example, beekeepers who read random bee blogs and ask random people for advice will very likely struggle with the process.

The right people to ask include experienced beekeepers with a proven track record of succeeding with their hives. Ask those who have made mistakes, learn from their errors, perform better, and ask those who give useful advice instead of speculations.

As a beginner, I recommend you should always seek knowledge and learn more about beekeeping, but be wary of unverified information. Always work with those who have made progress and can show you proof of their success. Those who are not competent and sincere will only have words for you: words without action will not be useful to you. This realization is why you shouldn't rely solely on what you read online from "Acclaimed beekeepers in your locality." Pay a visit and see for yourself before taking their word for it.

Equipment errors

A lot of beginners make equipment errors, which might mean using tools and supplies the wrong way, buying appliances based on the popularity of a brand instead of functionality, and many other errors. Some beekeepers use an insulating tool for winter that has a larger capacity than the hive, leading to too many bees.

Another equipment mistake entails buying cheap equipment because you want to save money and ending up with a very bad tool. If the equipment is too cheap to be true, then maybe it isn't true! It could be that the tools are unreliable. Or they might be unsterilized and bring diseases into your hive.

When buying tools, your first consideration should be for the quality of its functionality and not only the price. I know we all want to get a good deal on the price, but would you rather get a "good deal" and ruin your hive? Another way of preventing this mistake is to ask for help from experienced beekeepers who can advise on the kind of beekeeping tools to purchase and where to get the right products.

Another equipment error happens when beekeepers store tools in the wrong places. If you keep your beekeeping equipment in a filthy environment and use it to work on the hive, you will be exposing the bees to infection and diseases.

I have no doubt at all that you are a fantastic beekeeping beginner who is about to take over the beekeeping world and do it flawlessly! Please note that with the best of intentions and all the care there is, you may make some mistakes while beekeeping. If so, don't be too hard on yourself for making errors. Learn from the mistakes and keep going because even experienced beekeepers still get it wrong sometimes.

Well done, and I hope the information in this chapter will help you minimize or altogether avoid beginners' mistakes. With this chapter, we have come to the end of an exciting and "Honey-filled" journey! Let us round off this experience with a concluding section, which entails a call-to-action prompt that will cause you to get started on this beekeeping journey right away.

Final Words

Beekeeping can be a fun experience for anyone who takes the time to understand the process and implement it the right way. Yes, it is a peculiar animal nurturing process because the bees are fragile and sensitive. Still, when you are consistent and intentional with grooming bees, it will become a part of your routine.

You have just read through a comprehensive manual on how to groom bees, and I hope you have gleaned a lot of information that will inspire you to take action. Some people have started the beekeeping process and given up midway because they experienced a few challenges (Stings, pests, and diseases).

As a beginner, you will have to deal with these initial "First-year blues" as both you and the bees are trying to get comfortable in this new area. The bees are trying to get used to their new hive; you are trying to get used to taking care of them and being a conscientious beekeeper. As such, you shouldn't be so hard on yourself when you make some initial mistakes.

Become determined and ready to face the challenges and remember you can learn from all your mistakes. Always bear in mind that most of the solutions and ideas about beekeeping you read about today are information gathered by someone else who made a mistake with their beekeeping process. If that person had given up, they wouldn't know what works and what doesn't work.

The best step to take towards beekeeping is the first step, and after that, you will get better. Start with the first step: use what you have learned, get your hive, bees, and start beekeeping. You can always refer to this book if you have questions as you continue. I sincerely hope it will be a useful source of advice and information for you.

You started this fantastic journey by first understanding the fundamentals of beekeeping; then, you moved on to learn how to create a hive and install your bees. You also learned how to nurture and feed bees while discovering all about the different seasons. Pest and disease control were discussed in this book as well as cleaning the hive, tools needed, and avoiding mistakes.

Everything you need to get started is available; don't wait any longer! Now, if you already have a site for your hive, but it doesn't have flowers around it, you can hold off for a while before getting the hive and bees. While waiting, plant some flowers (you already have some suggestions in Chapter Four).

Planting the flowers before bringing the bees is a way of preparing your hive environment for successful beekeeping. Think about the last time you moved to a new home; you probably had to ensure you had the necessary amenities such as water and electricity before making the place home. Well, your bees are moving from where they are to where you are taking them: please make it feel like home, and they will work hard to give you a bountiful and honey-filled harvest.

Best wishes!

www.ingramcontent.com/pod-product-compliance
Lightning Source LLC
Chambersburg PA
CBHW050326120526
44592CB00014B/2063